W9-BWZ-854

STAY TRUE

ALSO BY HUA HSU

A Floating Chinaman: Fantasy and Failure Across the Pacific

STAY TRUE

A Memoir

HUA HSU

DOUBLEDAY ⚓ NEW YORK

Published in the United States by Doubleday,
a division of Penguin Random House LLC, New York,
and distributed in Canada
by Penguin Random House Canada Limited, Toronto.

www.doubleday.com

DOUBLEDAY and the portrayal of an anchor with a dolphin
are registered trademarks of Penguin Random House LLC.

Small portions of this book have previously appeared in much different
form in *The New Yorker, Dædalus, Lucky Peach,* and on NPR.com.

Jacket photograph © Anthony Chang
Jacket design by Oliver Munday

Library of Congress Cataloging-in-Publication Data
Names: Hsu, Hua, 1977– author.
Title: Stay true : a memoir / Hua Hsu.
Description: First edition. | New York : Doubleday, [2022]
Identifiers: LCCN 2021055618 (print) | LCCN 2021055619 (ebook) |
ISBN 9780385547772 (hardcover) | ISBN 9780593315200 (paperback) |
ISBN 9780385547789 (ebook)
Subjects: LCSH: Hsu, Hua, 1977—Childhood and youth. | Taiwanese
Americans—California—San Francisco Bay Area—Biography. |
Hsu, Hua, 1977—Friends and associates. | Popular culture—United
States—History—20th century—Anecdotes. | University of California,
Berkeley—Students—Biography. | Murder victims—California—
Berkeley—Biography. | Taiwanese Americans—Cultural assimilation—
Anecdotes. | Children of immigrants—California—Biography. |
Coming of age.
Classification: LCC F868.S156 H78 2022 (print) |
LCC F868.S156 (ebook) | DDC 979.4/67—dc23/eng/20211206
LC record available at https://lccn.loc.gov/2021055618
LC ebook record available at https://lccn.loc.gov/2021055619

MANUFACTURED IN THE UNITED STATES OF AMERICA
1 3 5 7 9 10 8 6 4 2

First Edition

For our parents
and for my friends

Only the future can provide the key to the interpretation of the past; and it is only in this sense that we can speak of an ultimate objectivity in history. It is at once the justification and the explanation of history that the past throws light on the future, and the future throws light on the past.

EDWARD HALLETT CARR, *What Is History?* (1961)

Because you're empty, and I'm empty
And you can never quarantine the past

PAVEMENT, "Gold Soundz" (1994)

STAY TRUE

B ACK THEN, there was no such thing as spending too much
time in the car. We would have driven anywhere so long as
we were together.

I always offered my Volvo. First, it seemed like the cool, generous thing to do. Second, it ensured that everyone had to listen
to my music. Nobody could cook, yet we were always piling
into my station wagon for aspirational trips to the grocery store
on College Avenue, the one that took about six songs to get to.
We crossed the Bay Bridge simply to get ice cream, justifying
a whole new mixtape. There was a twenty-four-hour Kmart
down 880 that we discovered one night on the way back from
giving someone a lift to the airport—the ultimate gesture of
friendship. A half-hour drive just to buy notepads or underwear
in the dead of night, and it was absolutely worth it. Occasionally, a stray, scratchy pop tune would catch someone's attention.
What's this? I'd heard these songs hundreds of times before. But
to listen to them with other people: it was what I'd been waiting for.

Passengers had different personalities. Some called shotgun
with a neurotic intensity, as though their entire sense of self
relied on sitting up front. Sammi flicked her lighter all the time,
until one afternoon when the glove compartment caught on
fire. Paraag always ejected my tapes and insisted on listening to
the radio. Anthony, forever staring out the window. You might
come no closer to touching another person than in a cramped
backseat, sharing a seat belt meant for one.

I had taken my parents' fear of blind spots to heart, and my head constantly bounded from side to side, checking the various mirrors, noting cars in neighboring lanes, in between sneaking glances to see if anyone else noticed that Pavement was far superior to Pearl Jam. I was responsible for my friends' safety, and for their enrichment, too.

I have a photo of Ken and Suzy sitting shoulder to shoulder in the back just as we're about to embark on a short road trip. They're chewing gum, smiling. I remember nothing about the trip except the excitement of leaving for someplace else. Finals were over, and before we went our separate ways for summer, a bunch of us spent the night at a house a few hours away from Berkeley. The fun, minor danger of driving in a caravan, as though on a secret mission, weaving through traffic, carefully looking in the rearview to see that everyone else was still behind you. Swerving from lane to lane or tailgating when we were the only cars on the road. I probably spent more time making the mixtape than it took to drive to the house and back. We wouldn't even be gone for twenty-four hours. But there was the novelty of sleeping bags, no homework, waking up in the morning somewhere unfamiliar and new, and that was enough.

In general, I wasn't used to seeing Ken in the backseat. We spent a lot of nights driving around Berkeley, his leg propped up on the passenger side door, his eyes scanning the horizon for undiscovered coffee shops, some out-of-the-way dive bar that would become our haunt once we turned twenty-one. He was always overdressed—a collared shirt, a Polo jacket, things I would never wear—but maybe it was just that he was ready for adventure. More often than not, a song's drive to 7-Eleven for cigarettes.

At that age, time moves slow. You're eager for something to happen, passing time in parking lots, hands deep in your pockets, trying to figure out where to go next. Life happened elsewhere, it was simply a matter of finding a map that led there. Or maybe, at that age, time moves fast; you're so desperate for action that you forget to remember things as they happen. A day felt like forever, a year was a geological era. The leap from sophomore to junior year of college suggested unprecedented new heights of poise and maturity. Back then, your emotions were always either very high or very low, unless you were bored, and nobody in human history had ever been this bored before. We laughed so hard we thought we'd die. We drank so much we learned there was a thing called alcohol poisoning. I always feared I had alcohol poisoning. We stayed up so late, possessed by delirium, that we came up with a theory of everything, only we forgot to write it down. We cycled through legendary infatuations sure to devastate us for the rest of our lives.

For a while, you were convinced that you would one day write the saddest story ever.

I remember listening to the Fugees. I remember the chill of the air. I remember the morning after, when everyone emerged from their own corner of the house, and Ken stepped out onto the deck, holding a mug of coffee. *How does he know how to make coffee?* I thought to myself. *I should know how to do that, too.* I have a photo of him still as he looks out toward the morning, clouds reflecting in his glasses. He wore glasses only on occasion, in a manner that made him seem serious, grown-up—never a nerd.

After breakfast—what could we have possibly eaten?—we ventured out to the white sand beach, though the weather was no good. I wore a thrift polka-dot button-up with a frayed collar, a brown cardigan, and a striped yellow-and-black beanie. Only my taupe Vans had been manufactured in our lifetime. There's a photo where I'm squatting down like a catcher, pen-

sively looking for seashells. Ken stands behind, leaning over me
and waving gaily to the camera. He wears a flannel-lined navy
blue jacket, tastefully baggy jeans, and brown boots. In another
picture, he's perched coolly on a tall rock. "Take one of me and
Huascene," he asks Anthony. He's affecting a debonair look,
while I'm leaning next to him with a goofy smile.

Back then, years passed when you wouldn't pose for a picture. You wouldn't think to take a picture at all. Cameras felt
intrusive to everyday life. It was weird to walk around with one,
unless you worked for the school paper, which made picture
taking seem a little less creepy. Maybe if you had a camera, you
used it during those last few days of school, at parties or as people were packing up, the logic of last-minute cramming applied
to the documentation of memories. If someone tried to take
your picture, even if it was meant to be silly or spontaneous, you
still fussed and awkwardly posed, because there was a finality
to it, one or two snaps at most, any more would seem obses-
sive. A moment would pass, unremarked upon, until months
later, when you developed photos you had taken at a concert
or birthday party, a proper event worth chronicling, and you
discovered some images of friends getting ready to go out, or
else a slice-of-life candid intended to burn through the end of
the roll. You'd forgotten about this. Later, when photography
became ubiquitous, pictures were evidence that you existed at
all, day in and day out. They registered a pattern. Looking back,
you began to doubt the sequence of events. If, in the absence of
proof, anything had happened at all.

Hello, Here is the answer :

$$y = (\underbrace{1.20 - 0.02X}_{\text{price}})(\underbrace{50 + X}_{\text{number}})$$

income

number of increasing
Sale

(number of ~~increasing~~)

$$= 60 + 1.2X - X - 0.02X^2$$

$$= 60 + 0.2X - 0.02X^2$$

draw a graph

60.5

60.0

At $1.2 - 0.02 \times 5 = 1.10$ per ice

her income will be maximum

at 60.5

$$y = 60 + 0.2x - 0.02x^2$$

~~60.2~~ ~~0.02 (x² -)~~

$$= 60 - 0.02(x^2 - 10x)$$

$$= 60 - 0.02[(x-5)^2 - 5^2]$$

60	1
60.18	2
60.32	
60.42	3
60.48	4
60.5	5
60.48	6
60.42	7
60.32	8
60.18	9
60	10

This year
World series
very exit...
wasn't it
Lot & sp
play and a
down to the
at every ex

D

W HEN MY FATHER MOVED to Taiwan, my family bought a pair of fax machines. In theory, this was so he could help me with my math homework. I was starting high school, where everything, from what instrument I played to the well roundedness of my transcript, suddenly seemed consequential. A few years earlier, in seventh grade, I tested *just* well enough to skip two years of math, and I was now paying for it. I had peaked too early. In fact, I was very bad at math. Like many immigrants who prized education, my parents retained faith in the mastery of technical fields, like the sciences, where answers weren't left to interpretation. You couldn't discriminate against the right answer. But I preferred to spend my time interpreting things.

Faxing was cheaper than long-distance calling, and far less pressure. There were no halting, wasteful silences. You simply dialed the recipient and fed a sheet of paper through the machine, and a facsimile printed out on the other side of the world. The time difference between Cupertino and Hsinchu was such that I could fax my father a question in the evening and expect an answer by the time I woke up. My homework requests were always marked urgent.

He carefully explained the principles of geometry in the margins, apologizing if anything was rushed or unclear, as he was very busy establishing himself at his new job. I skimmed the explanations and copied down the equations and proofs. Every now and then, I rewarded his quick, careful attention by interspersing the next set of math questions with a digest of

American news: I told him about Magic Johnson's announcement that he was HIV positive, I narrated the events that led up to the Los Angeles riots, I kept him up to date on the fate of the Giants. I told him about cross-country practice, made honest commitments to work harder at school. I listed the new songs I liked, and he would seek them out in Taipei's cassette stalls, and tell me which ones he liked, too:

> I like the November Rain by Guns N' Roses. The Metallica is also great. I couldn't enjoy the Red Hot Chili Peppers and Pearl Jam. The old songs reinterpreted by Mariah Carey (I'll Be There) and Michael Bolton (To Love Somebody) are marvelous. The MTV's "unplug" is a great idea!

As a teenager, I ultimately had better things to do than fax with my dad. He seized upon anything I mentioned and barraged me with questions. I described one of my classes as boring, and he interrogated my use of the term, observing "lots of 'challenges' are emotional 'boring' but reasonable 'useful.'" I mentioned that we were covering the 1960s in history class, and he asked, "You are convinced that Oswald alone killed JFK?"

He always asked me what I thought about things. Maybe it was his attempt to prolong our back-and-forth. He brought up sports, something I didn't think interested him at all. We were like two guys trading small talk at a hardware store.

> Redskin is too much for Bill!?

> How's the Nicks? [Knicks]

> It's Jordan vs. Buckley! [Barkley]

> This World Series was spectacular.

Whenever there was a weeklong break from school, my mom and I flew to Taiwan to see him. Sometimes, I tried to seem consumed by schoolwork so that maybe it made more sense for him to visit us in the Bay Area rather than us going all the way there. This never worked. We spent summers and winters in Hsinchu; weeks would pass when the only people I spoke to were my parents and their middle-aged friends.

I always dreaded these trips. I couldn't understand why my parents wanted to go back to a place they had chosen to leave.

My father left Taiwan for the United States in 1965, when he was twenty-one, and he'd be nearly twice as old before he set foot there again. In those days, you left if you were able, especially if you were a promising student. A dozen other physics majors graduated alongside him from Tunghai University, and ten of them ended up pursuing careers abroad. My father flew from Taipei to Tokyo to Seattle to Boston. He scanned the crowd for the friend who'd come all the way from Providence to pick him up at the airport and drop him off in Amherst.

But his friend didn't know how to drive, so he, in turn, promised to buy lunch for another guy, a man my dad didn't know, in exchange for a ride to the Boston airport, then Amherst, and finally back to Providence. The two young men greeted my father at the gate, traded backslaps, and rushed him to the car, where they stowed the sum total of his worldly possessions— textbooks and sweaters, mostly—in the trunk. Then they set off for Boston's Chinatown, a portal back to a world they had left behind. Camaraderie and goodwill were fine enough reasons to drive hours to fetch someone from the airport; just as important was the airport's proximity to food you couldn't get in small, northeastern college towns.

In the years that followed, a willing maroon far from home, my father acquired various characteristics that might have marked him as an American. He lived in New York, witnessed and participated in student protests, and, according to photographic evidence, once sported long hair and vaguely fashionable pants. He arrived as a devotee of classical music, but within a few years his favorite song was the Animals' "House of the Rising Sun." He subscribed very briefly to *The New Yorker,* before realizing it wasn't meant for newcomers like him and requesting a refund. He discovered the charms of pizza and rum raisin ice cream. Whenever new grad students were set to arrive from Taiwan, he and his friends piled into the nearest available car to pick them up. It was a ritual, and it was a type of freedom—on the road and possibly eating well—that was not to be passed up.

If Americans at the time knew anything about Taiwan, it was as an obscure island in the vicinity of China and Japan, where cheap plastic things were manufactured for export. When my mother was a child, her father set up a chalkboard in the family's kitchen where he would write a new word in English each day. World War II had interrupted my grandfather's medical studies, so he became a civil servant. He wanted slightly more for his children. My grandparents had my mom and her siblings choose American names, like Henry or Carol. The children picked up the basics of English, this bizarre, new language, which they might use to speak a new future into being. They learned about the rest of the English-speaking world through a subscription to *Life* magazine, where my mom first discovered the existence of something in America called Chinatown.

When she arrived in the United States in 1971 (Taipei–Tokyo–San Francisco), the family who picked her up had the decency to wait a day, so she could recover from the long jour-

ney, before taking her to eat Chinese food. She was on her way
to study public health at Michigan State. Soon after she got to
East Lansing, signed a lease, enrolled in classes, and bought
a stack of nonrefundable textbooks, she received a message
from her father. It turned out that as she was making her way
to Michigan, a letter had reached the family home in Taipei
informing her that she'd been accepted to the University of
Illinois at Urbana-Champaign, her top choice. So, my mother
recovered whatever tuition she could from Michigan State and
quickly departed for Illinois.

In the 1960s, communities of students from throughout
the Chinese-speaking world found one another in these small,
relatively remote college towns. Most of them adapted to the
changing seasons, a different register of conversational pleas-
antry, the rolling fields and endless highways. School anchored
my mother to the Midwest, but she roamed freely: a job at a
community center in Kankakee, where she was the only person who wasn't Black—her first up-close glimpse of America's
racial divide; a summer spent waitressing, where she ate ice
cream every day for lunch. But some of her classmates couldn't
deal with this radical new context, or maybe it was a lack of
one. She still remembers one girl who stopped going to classes
altogether, spending her time drifting around campus. Even at
the peak of summer, the girl wandered around, wearing her
heaviest winter coat. All the other Taiwanese students kept their
distance from her.

There were the potlucks with friends, when my mom would
make lion's head meatballs, road trips to famous landmarks or
grocers that carried bok choy, the bustling communion of dorm
life. You could identify a Taiwanese student by their Tatung rice
cooker. My mom took up painting, much of it abstract and sur-
real, color patterns that didn't reveal a discernible mood. When

I later asked if she'd been on drugs when she made them, she assured me she never smoked weed back then, even though she still remembered what it smelled like.

After two years at the University of Massachusetts Amherst, my father transferred to Columbia University. From there, he followed his academic adviser to the University of Illinois, which is where my parents met. They married at a student center on campus; if they had lived closer than three hours from the nearest Chinatown, they could have hosted a restaurant banquet. My mom's brother, who'd left Taiwan as a merchant marine and ended up in Virginia, was the only person from their combined families who was able to attend. At least they had their friends. One of them was an artist, and he drew pictures of Snoopy and Woodstock on cardboard and arranged them in the grass outside the student center. Everyone brought their favorite dish.

Immigrants are often discussed in terms of a push-and-pull dynamic: something pushes you from home; something else pulls you far away. Opportunities dry up one place and emerge somewhere else, and you follow the promise toward a seemingly better future. Versions of these journeys stretch back hundreds of years in all different directions.

In the nineteenth century, the British and Chinese were amicable trade partners, the British exchanging silver for China's tea, silk, and porcelains. But the British sought an advantage. They began cultivating opium in India and transporting it to China, where it was then transferred to smugglers who distributed it throughout the country. The Chinese eventually tried to wean themselves off the substance, stoking British fears that Chinese ports would one day be closed to them. The ensuing

Opium Wars devastated southeastern China, right around the time when cheap labor was needed in the American West. In the 1840s and 1850s, shiploads of Chinese men left the war-torn Guangdong province for the U.S., lured by promises of work. They laid railroad tracks, mined gold, and went wherever they were needed. Yet this was the limit of their mobility. Sequestered in the cities' most run-down districts by byzantine legal codes and social pressure—and without the means (and sometimes desire) to return home—they began building self-sustained Chinatowns to feed, protect, and care for one another. By the 1880s, the American economy no longer needed cheap foreign labor, resulting in exclusionary policies that limited Chinese immigration for decades.

These dynamics of push and pull were still in play when the Immigration Act of 1965 relaxed restrictions on entry from Asia, at least for people who might have something concrete to contribute to American society. There was a perception among policy makers that America was losing the science and innovation side of the cold war, so the country welcomed grad students like my parents. And who knew what the future held in Taiwan? In the New World, things seemed in a constant ascent. My parents weren't drawn to the United States by any specific dream, just a chance for something different. Even then, they understood that American life is unbounded promise and hypocrisy, faith and greed, new spectrums of joy and self-doubt, freedom enabled by enslavement. All of these things at once.

My parents took a long road trip from Illinois to the East Coast for their honeymoon, snapping photos along the way. The only real account of this trip comes back to them in flashes since they lost all the undeveloped rolls in Manhattan when someone broke into their car in broad daylight.

I was born in 1977 in Urbana-Champaign. My dad had wanted to become a professor. But after he couldn't find an academic job, we moved to Texas, where he worked as an engineer. The suburbs of Dallas afforded us plenty of space. One could get lost in that vastness. A few years ago, I found a small square of brittle, yellowed paper that dated back to the early 1980s—an ad my mom took out in the local classifieds:

CHINESE COOKING LESSONS—learn to Cook exotic
dishes using ingredients and utensils readily available.
$12 per class. For further information call Mrs. Hsu at:
867-0712

Nobody ever called. When I began speaking in a drawl, and begging for cowboy boots and an American name, and after they had been told that the local steak house wasn't for "their kind," they decided to try their luck elsewhere.

My parents' previous addresses are a history of friendships and acquaintances: a spare room in someone's attic, visits to family friends whom they'd only heard about but never actually met, a summer job in a small town a few hours away, a work opportunity in an unfamiliar, emerging field. They didn't dream of the big city so much as they mapped out proximities to friends, Chinese food, a good school district, a senior citizens' home. So, after Texas, it was either Delaware or California, and they chose California.

Cupertino was still in transition when we arrived in 1986. There was a huge factory downtown, farms, and a few Apple buildings that seemed a joke. Nobody used Apple computers.

Suburbs are about the leisurely conquest of space, an alternative to the uncomfortable density of the city. They seem to run free from history itself, offering a sense that nothing was there before. But the illusion of tranquility frays at the edges: the neurosis required to maintain so neatly manicured a lawn, the pristine sidewalks that nobody walks on, the holy wars fought to keep one municipality from oozing into the next. Suburbs suggest stability and conformity, yet they are rarely beholden to tradition. Rather, they are slates that can be wiped clean to accommodate new aspirations.

As Silicon Valley flourished in the late 1980s and early 1990s, more Asian immigrants moved to places like Cupertino. All of my grandparents relocated from Taiwan to the South Bay, and most of my parents' brothers and sisters settled there as well. Taiwan represented but a distant and imaginary former homeland. Silicon Valley's suburbs were amenable to a kind of meandering, gradual transformation; flagging businesses were remade by new waves of immigrants, while strip malls began turning, store by store, into crowded islands of Chinese food and the latest in asymmetrical hair art. There were bubble-tea cafés and competing Chinese bookstores, parking lots mazy with modified Hondas and moms hoping to preserve their pale complexions with full-face visors and sleeve-length driving gloves.

Vestiges of what stood before remained, the cycles of use and reuse: Cherry Tree Lane, where an actual orchard was once the best possible use of free acreage; the peaked roof of a former Sizzler turned dim sum spot; the kitschy railroad-car diner turned noodle shop. Chefs from Hong Kong and Taiwan joined the waves of engineers coming to California. The pressure to appeal to non-Chinese shoppers or diners casually disappeared. The concept of "mainstream" no longer held. Neck bones and chicken feet and various gelatinous things, VHS dubs of the latest Taiwanese dramas, Chinese-language newspapers and books: all could pay the bills and then some.

I realized how long my parents had been away from Taiwan when my mom began complaining about the newer immigrants from China—the way they would leave their shopping carts strewn about the parking lot of the Asian grocery store. The distinctions between a Taiwanese immigrant who came in the 1970s and someone who came from China in the 1990s were probably imperceptible to anyone outside the Chinese-speaking diaspora. They looked roughly the same, and they probably both had accents. But they also related differently to American culture and the question of where you fit within it. These new, ill-mannered immigrants probably didn't even know there was once but a single Asian grocer in the area, and it wasn't even that good, and you had to drive half an hour to get there.

Among the items that survived my parents' frugal early years are weathered paperback copies of the best sellers *Future Shock* and *The Pentagon Papers*. A pamphlet of Theodore Allen's essay "Class Struggle and the Origin of Racial Slavery: The Invention of the White Race" with "C. HSU" written across the cover. A book on Nixon's visit to China, another on African American history.

Maybe this was what it meant to live in America. You could move around. You were afforded opportunities unavailable back home. You could refashion yourself a churchgoer, a pizza lover, an aficionado of classical music or Bob Dylan, a fan of the Dallas Cowboys because everyone else in the neighborhood seemed to be one. For a brief spell, my father toyed with anglicizing his name and asked to be called Eric, though he soon realized that assimilation of that order didn't suit him. You were free to name your children after U.S. presidents. Or you might name them something unpronounceable, since they would never be president anyway.

From Amherst to Manhattan to Urbana-Champaign to Plano to Richardson to Mission Viejo to Cupertino: there were always the records, an old record player my father had soldered together himself, a pair of Dynatone speakers. He started building his music collection as soon as he arrived in America. At first, he used a mail-order LP club, the kind where you over-pay for a few, and then get a dozen more for a penny. It was mostly classical music back then. But he grew accustomed to Bob Dylan's strained rasp blasting from a neighbor's apartment sometime in the 1960s. He started buying Dylan records, learning to appreciate that voice, thin and weird, perhaps even more than he ever came to understand the words.

His records would stay protected in their original shrink-wrap, if possible, to avoid wear to the cardboard sleeve. He would peel back part of the plastic to stamp his name—Hsu Chung-Shih. Some of his records were given away over the years, but the core remained: Dylan, the Beatles and Stones, Neil Young, Aretha Franklin, Ray Charles. A few by the Who, Jimi Hendrix, Pink Floyd, some Motown collections. A lot of classical music. Blind Faith, because, when my parents were graduate students, an older faculty member from the West Indies had pulled out his violin during a dinner party to play the solo from "Sea of Joy." There were John Lennon and George Harrison solo albums, but none by Paul McCartney, so I assumed his post-Beatles career was awful. No Beach Boys meant they were probably awful, too. There was no jazz, except for a lone Sonny and Linda Sharrock album that's still sealed. They played *Thriller* so much that I assumed Michael Jackson was a family friend.

My father's record collection only had the effect of making music seem uncool to me. It was something that grown-ups took seriously. He listened to Guns N' Roses, whereas I listened to baseball games on the radio. He was the one recording hours of MTV on one VCR and whittling his findings down to a greatest hits tape on another VCR. He was the one who always wanted to go to Tower Records and browse the aisles, picking up old favorites in whatever new format was available. He bought *Rolling Stone* and *Spin* and carefully copied their lists of the year's or decade's best albums, and then he searched for the ones he thought he might enjoy.

Once I started middle school, I realized that my dad's record buying had prepared me for the social hierarchies of recess. I started watching MTV and listening to music on the radio, picking up on things early enough to never seem like a poseur, which I feared more than anything. I acquired the pop chart know-how that is the teenager's surest commodity by reading my dad's magazines and memorizing band names, reference points, miscellaneous trivia. And I now tagged along on his after-dinner trips to the record store. We seemed to spend hours apart, occasionally intersecting in some unlikely aisle. Everything seemed a possibility, a clue, an invitation to experience new, unprecedented emotional realities. We were enthralled by the same music, but it showed us different things. I listened to Slash's flamboyant, searching guitar solo on "November Rain" and heard liberation, a suggestion that crazed, committed vision could carry you away, somewhere else. To my parents, Slash's greatness was evidence of virtuoso skill, the product of thousands of hours of study and practice.

As Silicon Valley boomed in the early 1990s, so, too, did Taiwan's semiconductor industry. Soon, my parents' friends began moving back after decades away, maintaining homes in two countries so their children could finish high school and go to college in the States. By the late 1980s, my dad had risen to middle management in America. But he wearied of the corporate ladder, where advancement to the uppermost strata seemed tracked to arbitrary forces, like the color of one's skin, the subtle quivers in a voice. My parents eventually decided that he would move back to Taiwan, too. A job as an executive awaited him. Never again would he have to dye his hair or touch his golf clubs. We bought two fax machines.

I sometimes ran into classmates at the airport and realized that we were all there to drop our dads off at work. We lived in one of the only cities in America where this was not a hard arrangement to explain. It was a bit like the "Gold Mountain," a Chinese folktale of American opportunity that had endured since the gold rush. Except in those days, the men would cross the Pacific in search of work in America, not the other way around.

.   .   .

The first generation thinks about survival; the ones that follow tell the stories. I often try to spin the details and small effects of my parents' lives into a narrative. How did they acquire a sense of taste or decide which movies to see? Would they have recognized themselves in *Future Shock*? And who was the influential Eric in my father's life? The things around them were like the raw materials for new American identities, and they foraged as far as their car or the subway line could take them. Back then, it required a small fortune and months of careful planning to return home. It took weeks simply to schedule a long-distance phone call and ensure a quorum of the family would be available on the other end of the line.

They had come to study at American schools far superior to their Asian counterparts, though the reward for such a mad pursuit had yet to come into focus. They had chosen the occasional loneliness, the meandering lifestyle, the language barrier. What they hadn't chosen was identification as Asian Americans, a category that had only been coined in the late 1960s. They had little in common with the American-born Chinese and Japanese students organizing on the other side of their campuses for free speech or civil rights; they knew little about the Chinese Exclusion Act, Charlie Chan, or why one should take deep offense to a slur like "Oriental" or "Chink." My parents and their cohorts wouldn't have recognized that they were representatives of a "model minority." In fact, they hadn't even planned on becoming Americans. They simply didn't know such identities were available to them. Their allegiances remained to the world they had left behind.

How sweet and musical those phone calls must have been. What was it like for them to leave home and cross the Pacific, with only the haziest plans for return? In the absence of available connections, they held on to an imaginary Taiwan, more an abstraction—a beacon, a phantom limb—than an actual island. The available technology delivered them there only on special occasions. So, they searched for traces of home in the faces of their classmates; they heard it wafting above the din when they shopped for groceries.

Now my parents were free to come and go as they wished. My mother spent a lot of the 1990s on airplanes. They learned about Taiwan all over again. We lived in Hsinchu, a small coastal town about forty minutes south of Taoyuan Airport. Hsinchu was mainly known for its gusting winds and seafood meatballs. It was still slow and sleepy, only there was now a large high-tech campus off the highway, where all the semiconductor companies were headquartered. Giant malls started popping up downtown.

On weekends, my parents drove to Taipei to seek out old tea shops and movie theaters they remembered from the 1950s and 1960s. They didn't need maps. Decades away hadn't dulled their memory of which stalls served the best *baos*. My parents grew younger in Taiwan; the humidity and food turned them into different people. I sometimes felt like an interloper as we sat on weathered, wooden stools and silently ate giant bowls of beef noodles that, were this America, would have prompted a romantic soliloquy about their childhood memories.

I spent two or three months of every year in Taiwan. I always insisted on listening to ICRT, an English-language radio station, for Casey Kasem's *American Top 40* show, which offered weekly dispatches from a more recognizable reality. My parents had fond memories of listening to the station as teenagers, back when it was part of the Armed Forces Network. Over time, my father lost interest in new music, and listening to the countdown was partly my attempt to connect with him, to remind him of the American splendors to which he might one day return. It took me a while to understand that this was our life now—that my parents had worked hard in order to have a place in both worlds. Becoming American would remain an incomplete project, and my father's record collection began to seem like relics of an unfollowed path.

There's a telos of self-improvement baked into the immigrant experience. As a teenager, I busied myself with the school newspaper or debate club because, unlike with math or science, I thought I could actually get better at these things. You flip through your father's old physics notebooks, and you know in your bones that these formulas and graphs will never make sense to you. But one day, you realize that your parents speak with a mild accent, and that they have no idea what passive voice is. The next generation would acquire a skill on their behalf— one that we could also use against them. Commanding the language seemed like our only way of surpassing them. Home life took on a kind of casual litigiousness. The calm and composed children, a jaunty bounce to our sentences, laying traps with our line of questioning. The parents, tired and irritated, defaulting to the native tongue.

I spent a lot of time with my mom. She drove me all over the South Bay to cello lessons, cross-country meets, debate tournaments, record stores, listening as I regaled her with the minute details of my life. In return, I waited patiently with a stack of magazines whenever she went shopping for blouses or shoes. She watched whatever weird movies I brought back from the library, and she taught me how to shave. Every Friday, we went to Vallco, our local mall, starting at Sears and working our way to the food court for dinner. If anyone in a store wanted to talk to you, she said, you replied, as cheerfully as possible, "I'm just browsing," and they left you alone. I would explain what everyone else was wearing at school, and then we would figure out where you could possibly buy that stuff.

There comes a moment for the immigrant's child when you realize that you and your parents are assimilating at the same time. Later, I understood that we were both sifting, store to store, for some possible future—that we were both mystified by the same fashions, trends, and bits of language. That my late-night trips to the record store with my dad had been about discovery, not mastery. Later still, I came to recognize that assimilation as a whole was a race toward a horizon that wasn't fixed. The ideal was ever shifting, and your accent would never be quite perfect. It was a set of compromises sold to you as a contract. Assimilation was not a problem to be solved but the problem itself.

Like millions of other people, my first glimpse into the prospect of "alternative" culture came when I listened to Nirvana's "Smells Like Teen Spirit" in 1991. I was thirteen. It was one of the greatest songs I had ever heard, mostly because it was the first great song I had chosen on my own.

I believed that I'd happened upon a secret before everyone else, and I was addicted to this feeling. I heard the song late one night on the radio. The next day, nobody knew what I was talking about. There wasn't even a video yet. I patiently awaited the release of *Nevermind.*

At the time, I didn't know that "alternative" was a marketing concept, or that Nirvana had an album before *Nevermind.* I was clueless that *Nevermind* was the result of a major label bidding war. My only guide was my exhilaration. I remember staring at the tape deck as I listened to the album for the first time, amazed that each song seemed better than the last. And I was mystified by the way they chose to express themselves, undermining their own, innately catchy songs with layers of menacing noise or mischievous snarls. I carefully studied any magazine and newspaper articles I could find about them, copying down the references they made to other bands. I wrote a letter to the fan club listed in the cassette's booklet expressing my singular grasp of their values.

One day, Nirvana was a relatively obscure band from an unfancied part of the country. Then everyone saw the light. Kids at school began showing up with the same Nirvana T-shirt, puffy yellow ink on black. Was this a sign that the same secret could be cherished by everyone? That we would remake the world in our own image?

I was drawn to Nirvana mostly because they didn't seem like a bunch of morons. They made everything else on MTV appear barbaric and instantly irrelevant. Mainstream rock music fit within a limited gradient of American machismo, from fun-loving buffoons to the serious and virtuosic. Nirvana represented everything else; the fringe territories were infinite. When Kurt Cobain, their lead singer, was young, he read an article about punk rock and concluded that this was the music for him. It was the mid-1970s, and it would be a while until he actually heard any punk records. He later recalled being disappointed that the music wasn't as aggressive or vital as he'd imagined it. His own, imagined version of punk drove the band's career. He seemed hell-bent on redirecting his newfound fans toward the music he loved: Shonen Knife, the Raincoats, the Vaselines. He led us down a trail, pointing us toward out-of-the-way landmarks. Casting about for those other territories became my reason for being.

Naturally, the day came when far too many classmates were wearing Nirvana shirts. How could everyone identify with the same outsider? It wasn't the band's fault. Cobain seemed nonchalant, even hostile, toward his fame. I couldn't blame him for the adoration foisted upon him. He was, after all, good-looking and charismatic. But I would ensure that I'd never be like the poseur in my civics class who started humming "Smells Like Teen Spirit" and then singing the words "And it smells like / teen spirit." Everybody knows that's not how the song goes.

I began making a zine because I'd heard it was an easy way to get free CDs from bands and record labels. But it was also a way to find a tribe. My worldview was defined by music. I cultivated a pose that was modest and small, sensitive and sarcastic, skeptical yet secretly passionate. I scoured record stores and mail-order catalogs for 7-inch singles that sounded quiet and loud at the same time. I thought I had a lot to say, but I felt timid about saying it. Making my zine was a way of sketching the outlines of a new self, writing a new personality into being. I was convinced that I could rearrange these piles of photocopied images, short essays, and bits of cut-up paper into a version of myself that felt real and true. It was a kind of dream about what the future could hold—something that came into focus with every pun-filled, reference-packed sentence. Of course, there were many sentences that I couldn't yet write.

I used primitive page-layout software I'd persuaded my mom to buy because it would help me with college applications. Using four or five fonts per page communicated the sense of emotional chaos I hoped to project. I illustrated my zine with collages using images ripped out of driver's education manuals, magazines, Chinese textbooks. I wrote a lot about music, but I could have been zealous about anything—film, literature, art. I fell in love with anything I felt I had discovered. I wrote long, admiring essays about Pavement and Polvo because those were the first LPs I bought on my own after finally getting my driver's license, and I listened to those records obsessively until everything strange and dissonant about them began to sound normal. But I could have started browsing in the *R* section instead and fallen under the spell of other bands just as easily. What I prized was seriousness. I wanted to apply it to some small world, hidden in this larger one.

My zine was earnest yet cynical. *Wasn't this thing that had fallen out of fashion actually great? Why does everyone dress this way, rather than that?* I would write breathless odes to foreign films I'd never seen, passionate and overlong dissections of whatever 7-inch indie rock singles I could find at Streetlight in San Jose. There was *X-Files* fan fiction, screeds against our rote homework assignments. But I saw coolness as a quality primarily expressed through erudite discernment, and I defined who I was by what I rejected, a kitchen-sink approach to negation that resulted in essays decrying *Beverly Hills, 90210*, hippies, private school, George Bush, braided leather belts, the police state, and, after they became trendy, Pearl Jam. I knew what I was against, but I couldn't imagine what stood on the other side.

Maybe those were the last days when something could be truly obscure. Not in the basic sense that a style or song might be esoteric. But there was a precariousness to out-of-the-way knowledge, a sense that a misfiled book or forgotten magazine could easily be lost forever. Learning about something a few minutes before everyone else converted to a kind of niche social capital, and I was a diligent scholar. I knew all the bands that sounded a bit like Nirvana that nobody had heard of yet. I prized research: the excavation of arcane tributaries, secret knowledge, and conspiratorial anecdotes, building new religions around has-beens or never-weres.

I explored the less trafficked aisles of the comic shop, rummaged through my grandparents' apartment for old flannels, mohair ties, factory lab coats. I'd beg my mom to drive me to Berkeley, marveling at the college students as they angled enormous slices of pizza into their mouths, novels, notebooks, and records tucked under their arms. Any magazine article about cyberpunks, ravers, or animal rights activists suggested a new, totally plausible path for me. It was exciting to meander and choose who you wanted to be, what aspects of yourself to accent and adorn. You were sending a distress signal, hoping someone would come to your rescue.

It's hard enough to read tone in writing, and maybe even more so with a fax, which is printed on smooth thermal paper. You can't make out the imprint of the pen. Faxes arrive with a faded and distant look, the advice already ancient. My dad was curious about my zine (which he referred to as my "publications") and asked if I could fax a copy to him. I explained that it wouldn't be the same.

He often implored me to apply some of the energy I spent memorizing sports statistics or writing record reviews to my schoolwork. I just had to study my textbooks the way I studied my cherished magazines. I could tell you what albums were slated for release next month, but I couldn't, for the life of me, pass the written portion of the driver's test. "Don't take this as a negative comment. Only we love you and know your weakness, so we like to guide you. Your goodness and strong points are always in our hearts although we are not always saying them." Whenever he wrote something that came across sterner than intended, he quickly followed up, unprompted, to clarify:

Last Friday, I overemphasized the toughness. Don't be scared. The life is full of excitement and surprises. Handle it and enjoy it. Just like you said that you like the cross country exercise. After climbing the hill, looking downward, you feel good. That is the point I would like to make. Don't feel frustrate climbing climbing, also don't pick a too high mountain to climb in begin with. You need drill the small hill first. Learn from the exercise. Even a tumble can teach you how to climb next time. It's sweating, but enjoy the process.

Mom and I have been proud of you. Not only on your accomplishment but more on your happy personality. We'll support you whatever you choose (most time! Ha!). Don't feel bad if sometimes we are too nervous. We just hope to give you all our guidance and help to make your decisions simpler. We might put too much pressure on you but that's not what we mean. Be relax but arrange your time to handle priorities.

I feel sorry that I cannot be around all the time to support you whenever you need. But I feel comfortable since mom can do good job and you are quite mature. But if there is any thoughts

or problem, call me or fax to me. If it's class work and you cannot get my timely help, please tell us. We can arrange some
tutoring. 10th and 11th grade take more sweat but I hope you
enjoy them.

Love, Dad

The tutors didn't really help. They were usually twentysome-
thing immigrants from Taiwan studying at the local community
college. My haplessness at abstract math concepts was so deep-
rooted that they often had no idea where to begin with me. I
would scrutinize the way they dressed and spoke, and wonder
if this is what my parents had been like decades ago.

By junior year, I'd finished every math class my high school
offered, sustaining damage to my GPA along the way. But I
was now free to devote myself fully to the school paper, my
zine, and the debate club. I figured that I had to be really
good at these other things to make up for all the Cs on my
transcript.

One day, my dad faxed me. It was raining in Hsinchu. "California's sunny day also influence the 'thinking and behavior.' Make
people thinking 'bright.' Do you think so?" I didn't get why he was
always writing me about my moods. Maybe he was concerned
that I would succumb to the American disease of boredom, or
worse.

It felt a little anticlimactic when Kurt Cobain died in April 1994.
We had already mourned his passing the month before. Someone had heard that he died of an overdose while on tour in Italy,
and the rumor spread through my high school. We didn't find

out until the next day that Cobain was still alive, by which point we had already cycled through various stages of grief. I was in journalism class, and I cut a picture of him out of a magazine and glued it to a pin, declaring that I would wear it for the rest of my life.

When Cobain really did die, I wasn't particularly surprised because his health had seemed so precarious in the preceding years. He often spoke of his debilitating stomach issues. A history of depression ran through his family. The pressures of fame and all the nonstop touring seemed to exacerbate whatever it was he was feeling. His ragged voice and hunched frame weren't just affectations; they were physical manifestations of his discomfort. It's said that his heroin addiction became a coping mechanism for all of this. He died of a self-inflicted gunshot wound at his home in Seattle. His passing seemed instantly significant, like when our history teacher subjected us to stories about Kennedy's assassination. Cobain had been representative of something, but maybe not something of which I felt a part. He was outside the system, only I felt further outside it. I faxed my dad the night it happened. I couldn't understand Cobain's death by suicide. My dad wrote back:

Kurt's death was also on 7pm news here. I heard it in Uncle "Spock's" home during dinner time. It's sad. Right now, MTV has a special to pay the memory.

I agree it's a society tragedy, too much pressure. If he felt that it's beyond his control or creativity or else, it sometimes led to the conclusion of suicide, especially for talented artists. He felt that the sense of living disappeared. So sometimes, the "normal" people is more easy to adapt to the reality which fills with not ideal situation and needs compromise. That's the dilemma of life: you have to find meaning, but by the same time, you have to accept the reality. How to handle the contradiction is a challenge to everyone of us. What do you think?

After his death, there were articles and news segments about Cobain's nihilism, and what his choice suggested about America's youth. Even though he grew too popular for me to covet a T-shirt, I made a scrapbook of articles about Cobain. I answered one of the prompts on my French AP exam with a diatribe about what society had done to Cobain, praising the stand he had taken against racism, sexism, and homophobia. It was *tragique* that we swallowed him whole. I failed the exam. Clearly, the establishment would never understand us.

His was a persona that was more thoughtful, conflicted, and unguarded than those we were used to seeing. Maybe what I mistook for coolness was unease, a fear of growing too vulnerable. Maybe you can never be loved for the reasons you think you should be loved. Maybe the seeds of your rebellion will always be forgotten.

A couple weeks later, I faxed my dad a copy of an article I wrote for the school paper about Cobain's death and what it said about our generation. I was using the term loosely, since Cobain was ten years older than me. I believed there was something exceptional about our time, the pressures we faced, the struggles to remain content in aimless times. There were all these terms that seemed unique to us, like "dysfunction," "dystopia," and "angst." I tried them on, but nothing stuck. I watched the news and saw fans dressed in black, maintaining a vigil in a park near his house, crying for days in the arms of strangers. That was a deeper level of feeling I couldn't grasp. Still, I was a persuasive enough writer to concern my father.

I think your article do have many good points. Important one is whether a person is loving the life or sometimes hates himself and can not take it. Every generation has its own problem. For the young, being idealistic and feeling helpless at the same time is normal and necessary for the society to progress. But the problem is that life is and has to go on. Every generation has to face the problem and live through and try its best to overcome the frustration. In the 60's, society is quite rich but the immoral Vietnam War triggers the problem. Liberal thinking is a positive force for the society. Desegregation, human right, and anti-war were also very "frustrating" situation. Some survived and still active like Joan Baez, Bob Dylan, Neil Young. Some didn't, like Hendrix, Joplin, and Morrison.

What I want to say is that we have to have ideal thinking, heart, feeling about the society, environment, etc. But we also need to accept that there must have a way to change the world, or surrounding, to be better. It might take many years, or even generations, or many deaths. But still, emotion alone will not change the situation. Real work will. Kurt is talent. No doubt about it. And he is important. His death need to be analyzed very seriously. Our society to have problems. But don't paint the generation with stereotype such as "lost." I think that's true for all generations during a certain period of their life.

What do you think? In reading your article, I found that my English is very poor. What's the meaning of "dysfunction"?

Again, we have to have emotion that differentiate human being with machine, robot. But we also need to know how to control it and will not be carried away by it. Do you agree?

．　．

I was sixteen, and I wanted to be carried away. I would leave for college the next fall. I fantasized about going somewhere strange and new. Los Angeles wasn't far enough. San Diego was lame. Seattle was far enough but in a useless direction. I didn't like the idea of being landlocked. I felt too young for New York. Boston was lame, too. I was drawn to Johns Hopkins until I realized I wouldn't be nearly as enamored with a school called "John Hopkins." Actually, the novelty of flying had evaporated after one too many trips across the Pacific. My dad wanted me to start considering my options. "Berkeley is a good school with a good campus," he wrote. It was affordable, close to home, and less elitist than the "Ivory Tower" schools back east, not that it would be an issue if I wanted to apply to those schools, too. The only drawback, he explained, was its "neighborhood." He wasn't just talking about Oakland, though that was certainly part of it. Berkeley wasn't a bubble, like nearby Stanford. The campus bled into the world around it—the gnarly street punks and homeless people who lived in People's Park, the hippie burnouts who still wandered Telegraph. Just a few years earlier, in 1990, someone had taken hostages at a campus bar, leading to an all-night standoff with the local police. One student died and several were shot before the person was killed.

Life had delivered my parents thousands of miles away from their families. They had turned the other cheek, made the most of bad situations, answered to close-enough versions of their name. Then it somehow took them back to where they had come from, only, by then, their families had slowly moved away to be closer to one another in the Bay Area. My parents craved a kind of routine stability as they whittled the risk and variables out of their lives. They wanted me to acquire recognizable skills; they wanted me to be just accomplished enough to seem well-rounded. Berkeley was a good school with a good campus; on this point, we agreed. But I was desperate to go there because of the enormous slices of pizza, the left-wing bookstore tucked inside the parking garage, the weirdos yelling about free speech or abortion on the quad. I was matriculating into a world of abundance, where there was at least three of everything—used bookstores, record stores, vintage boutiques—within a four-block radius.

I was an American child, and I was bored, and I was searching for my people.

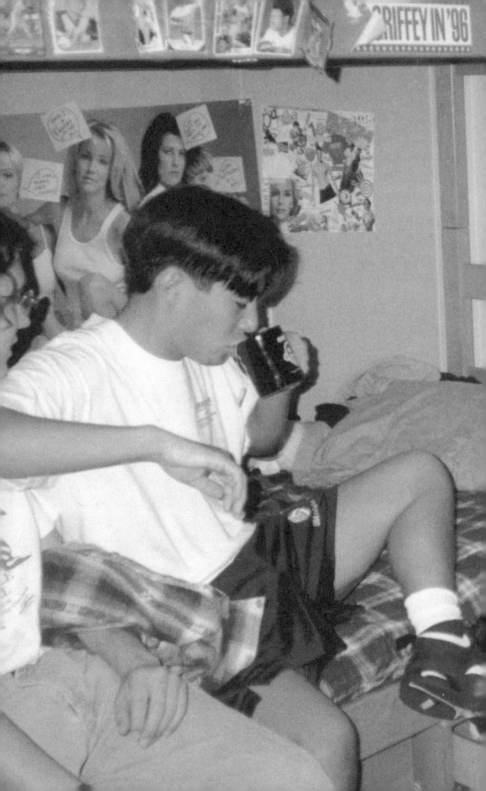

DURING THE FIRST couple weeks of college, everyone traveled in packs. A dormitory floor's worth of strangers wandering the video store, collectively trying to decide on a movie to rent. At a café all the way up Bancroft, eight freshmen huddled around a table meant for two, copying whatever the person before you in line ordered to drink. *I'll have a mocha, too.* There were rumors of an even better burrito spot than the one on Haste, but you had to take the bus. Before that: learn how to take the bus. Picking up on nicknames and reputations of various dorms, passing this knowledge off as your own. *They call that one Bosnia.* Trying in vain to peel fellow freshmen away from the herd to check out the record store instead.

Mostly, there were parties. We walked up Durant Avenue, past Telegraph, past Tower and Top Dog, toward Greek row, where the various fraternities and sororities offered the incoming first-years free beer, ready-made friend groups, and the chance to reinvent themselves. I would walk up the hill but never stayed at the parties for more than a few minutes. I identified as straight edge—a term I picked up from an older kid in high school.

Straight edge was a hard-core punk subculture that emerged in the early 1980s, premised on the principled, quasi-political rejection of drugs, alcohol, cigarettes—vices that could be taken to a banal extreme. I knew none of this at the time. I knew only that being straight edge involved listening to music that was loud and preachy, and casting judgment on anyone who was having too much fun. This seemed vaguely rebellious to me. A showy, disciplined zig to everyone else's sloppy zags.

I lived in a triple in Ida Sproul Hall with Paraag and Dave, two close friends from high school. Paraag's dad went to Berkeley for grad school in the 1960s, and they drove to campus early on move-in day so the family could take a picture of him on the steps of the campus's main plaza. His father had posed for a similar picture when he'd arrived from India.

I got to campus last that day, so I was stuck with the top bunk, above Paraag. Dave's bed was lofted above a long desk the two of them shared. They let me have the stand-alone desk that faced the window. Each of us became synonymous with whatever poster we had put up on our patch of wall: "The Women of *Melrose Place*" for Paraag, Batman for Dave. I bought a too-big Björk poster that I had to tape to the ceiling, just inches above my bed. Her head was the size of my entire mattress; I slept under the poster for a few days before it started to scare me and I took it down.

We had chosen to live together in order to ease the transition into college life, though we might have reconsidered this had we known that our triple would be smaller than a double. Paraag and Dave spent a lot of their free time exploring the gym and playing basketball. They wanted to major in business. I wasn't sure what I wanted to do besides looking for records.

I began sorting my classmates according to their musical sensibilities. Of secondary concern was someone's taste in film and books, what posters were on their walls, whether they knew about zines or thrifted their clothes. According to my blunt typology of the world, there were people who were cool and then people who weren't. This latter category was multitudinous. I was into being *into things,* and I sought this quality in others. It could have been anybody, anything. There was the Indian dude with the weathered mechanic's jacket who tried to get me into artsy, obscure metal, the red-haired girl in my English class who nearly convinced me that I could fall deeply in love with ska. Maybe I would become a proper punk. A Berkeley sophomore whom I knew from high school debate invited me to a Groovie Ghoulies show at 924 Gilman, only I had no idea who they were or how to get there. Even being straight edge was just evidence of susceptibility—of a desire to be folded into someone else's misfit gang. This was the reinvention I sought.

When you're young, you are certain of your capacity to imagine a way out of the previous generation's problems. There is a different way to grow old, paths that don't involve conforming and selling out. We would figure it out together, and we would be different together. I just had to find people to be different with, a critical mass of others to flesh out the possibilities of a collective pronoun.

The first time I met Ken, I hated him.

Ken lived too loud a life, at least by my standards. I had met hundreds of him, hundreds of times before. I was eighteen, in love with my moral compass, perpetually suspicious of anyone whose words came too easily. He was a genre of person I actively avoided—mainstream. Ken was flagrantly handsome; his voice betrayed no insecurity. He lived on the fourth floor, just above us, and his room was filled with reminders of who he had been in high school. A photo of his girlfriend back home, white and blond and conventionally pretty. One of him with his friends, dressed up like refs, heckling their crosstown rivals at a basketball game. He had good manners, which served him well at his after-school job selling children's shoes at a department store. He was adept at charming both sticker-shocked parents and their impatient children. He could treat a hangover, and he opened the door for others. He knew how to order at restaurants. He seemed eager for adult life.

High school had been a dream for Ken, and there were few signs that college would be any different. He hoped to become an architect. During the first week of school, he was tapped by a fraternity up the hill—the "most diverse one," he pointed out. They were grooming him for a leadership position. Pearl Jam and Dave Matthews Band—music I found appalling—boomed through their house. The brothers wore their baseball caps backward. There were always plastic cups everywhere.

Now that I was a college student, I tried to rebrand myself as someone who was outspoken, hopefully in a charmingly digressive way. Someone who knew a little about everything and fancied weighing in on stuff; this was how I hoped I came across when writing my zine. At the very least, I wanted to seem as if I were comfortable with my voice. My first class in college had about five hundred other students. You instantly realized the challenge of retaining whatever sense of uniqueness got you here in the first place. My smallest one was a seminar in the Peace and Conflict program, where our first homework assignment was to spend a week resisting the impulse to blame anyone else for anything.

I liked my English class, so I practiced reading poems aloud, because a professor said we would never understand poetry otherwise, and I desperately wanted to be the kind of person who understood poetry. One day, early in the semester, I mustered up the courage to raise my hand. Forty other prospective English majors turned to me as I riffed through an observation about Ernest Hemingway's use of naming. A sophomore told me I was wrong; the graduate instructor gravely nodded in agreement. I decided that literary interpretation wasn't for me and focused on political science instead. I reverted to being the type of student who avoided putting himself out there. I sat near the back, listening intently, seldom saying a word.

Ken was often on the third floor of our dorm, because unlike the fourth, where he lived, ours was coed. He'd come down to organize everyone to go to a party or to study in our lounge, since it had a balcony. Sometimes, he'd come to our room to check his email, which everyone treated as a dumb, bureaucratic encumbrance. We all knew each other's email passwords, and once or twice a week, when nobody was using the phone line, someone logged on to the desktop PC, which Dave's father had built for him, to check everyone's in-boxes. I never sent any messages, so I never got any, which bothered me, only I would never openly admit it. But it was obvious to Ken, who would yell for me to hurry back to my room, just so he could tell me that he and Paraag were checking email and that my in-box was still empty.

I was quiet, and Ken was loud. He projected confidence. I found confident people suspicious. He asked questions out of earnest curiosity, and I asked questions that were skeptical or coolly condescending. Mostly, I never wanted to let on when I didn't know something. *Oh yeah, I've heard of them.*

On Fridays, I'd take the bus to a shop on University that specialized in records imported from the UK. I'd spend hours there, flipping through the newest singles, trying in vain to make conversation with the unimpressed clerks. I interpreted their brusqueness as a higher level of coolness. They swept me away if I asked about some new release I spied behind the counter. That record's not for sale, they would say, at least not to me. Their regulars had first dibs. I aspired to become a regular.

I would return from my University excursions and see Ken, soaking in his gym clothes, sitting at my desk, using my prized *Teen Beat* mug. He, Paraag, and Dave would have just returned from playing basketball at the gym. He would refer to me as Huascene—my email address, adapted from a Blur song called "Popscene." Or he'd call me "Homecoming King," saying it in a way where you could hear the air quotes. Ken had a hard time believing that our high school had been so enlightened and weird that everyone protest voted me atop the popularity contest. He was boisterously overfamiliar, and I could never tell if he was making fun of me.

Californians often grow up with a sense of entitlement simply because they get to live in California. It's where people dream of ending up. There's always been a mutual suspicion between people from Northern and Southern California, and 99 percent of the people at Berkeley seemed to be from one or the other. The only unifying element was that everyone wore Adidas slides. I thought people from Southern California were superficial and unserious. They spent too much time in the sun. Where the Bay Area was known for politics and counterculture, they were known for Disneyland and Hollywood. It sounded ditzy the way they referred to the highway that ran through the state as *the* 101 rather than just 101. Ken had grown up in El Cajon, a suburb of San Diego, and he made it sound like a singular, golden place. Close to the beach, perfect weather, the nicest people, the prettiest girls. It sounded hellish and generic to me. I didn't even bother pointing out that the great rock critic Lester Bangs had grown up in El Cajon back in the 1960s. There was *no way* he'd heard of Lester.

Ken's father sold insurance; his mom would make me a life-changing feast of steaks and chicken if I ever came down to visit. He admired his older sister, even if he delighted in never communicating this to her directly. They doted on a squeaky, aggressive Pomeranian named Chibi. They sounded like a typical, all-American family, bright and optimistic in a way I found suspect.

My wariness about Ken was compounded by the fact that he was Asian American, like me. All the previous times I had met poised, content people like Ken, they were white. It's one of those obscure parts of an already obscure identity that Japanese American kids can seem like aliens to other Asians, untroubled, largely oblivious to feeling like outsiders. They gave those feelings up long ago. Japanese American families like Ken's have often been in the country for several generations. The children of recent immigrants feel discomfort at a molecular level, especially when doing typical things, like going to the pizza parlor on a Friday night, playacting as Americans. We are certain you've forgotten our names. The Japanese Americans I'd grown up around had parents who were into football and fishing, grandparents whose stories of the internment camps were recited with no trace of accent. Some of them had never even been to Japan, and some, too, had family who fought against Japan in World War II. We all look alike, until you realize we don't, and then you begin feeling that nobody could possibly seem more different.

.   .   .

There are many currencies to friendship. We may be drawn to someone who makes us feel bright and hopeful, someone who can always make us laugh. Perhaps there are friendships that are instrumental, where the lure is concrete and the appeal is what they can do for us. There are friends we talk to only about serious things, others who only make sense in the blitzed merriment of deep night. Some friends complete us, while others complicate us. Maybe you feel as if there were nothing better in the world than driving in a car, listening to music with friends, looking for an all-night donut shop. Nobody says a thing, and it is perfect. Maybe your lifelong fascination with harmony finally began to make sense in those scenes, packed in your family's station wagon, singing along to "God Only Knows," waiting in the parking lot until the song was over. Aristotle remarked that friendships among the young always orbit the possibility of pleasure. The lives of the young, he observed,

> are guided by emotion, and they pursue most intensely what they find pleasant and what the moment brings. As they advance in years, different things come to be pleasant for them. Hence, they become friends quickly and just as quickly cease to be friends. For as another thing becomes pleasant, the friendship, too, changes, and the pleasure of a young man changes quickly.

What the moment brings: that forward-facing dimension of friendship, the knowledge that you will grow old, or apart, and that you may one day need each other in some presently unimaginable way. We learn as children that friendship is casual and transient. As a structure, it's rife with imbalance, invisible tiers, pettiness, and insecurity, stretches when we simply disappear. For some, friendship needs to be steady and rhythmic. For others, it's the sporadic intimacy of effortlessly resuming conversations or inside jokes left dormant for years.

But before all that: a moment that brings you together.

The first time I *actually* met Ken, he asked me to help him buy clothes. Students had returned to campus after winter recess; Irami and I were hanging out in the lobby of our dorm. I politely nodded at Ken as he walked in with two suitcases. The elevator that serviced the building's eight floors was broken, as usual, and he sighed, but in a gallant, movie star way where his inconvenience was just part of the day's role. Irami, an aggressively thoughtful philosophy major who lived on my floor, tapped me on the shoulder. "Let's help him out." I seethed inside. There were people in our dorm I wanted to befriend, where the inertia of proximity, I was certain, would one day result in closeness. I'd find an empty seat in the dining hall and admire your thrift shop T-shirt, your ironic pin; maybe we'd start going to see bands together. Perhaps we would cross paths in the foreign section of the video store; I would stay up late, listening to your problems, and then I'd share my secrets in return. I'd spent enough time in Ken's periphery during the fall to conclude that he wasn't one of these people. He seemed so self-assured and normal, nothing drew me to him. I grabbed a suitcase and did my best to huff and puff as theatrically as possible as we went up the stairs. I didn't even like this person, and now I was doing physical labor for him.

When we got upstairs, Ken thanked us. He swiveled toward me and asked, "Where do you get your clothes?" He dressed well, in a ruggedly generic way, a Polo in a nonobvious color, casually tucked into his baggy jeans. Nikes or, when it was wintertime, Timberlands. I dressed like a grandfather—scratchy cardigans, floral button-downs, an audible amount of corduroy, Dr. Martens five-eye wingtips. I figured he was making fun of me. But he was serious. "Can you help me shop for a party at my house?"

I had no interest in parties, and I could think of nothing less cool than frat houses. But I was surprised, even impressed, by Ken, since he was clearly more perceptive than I'd initially thought. He noticed intentionality where others might have guessed I could only afford mismatched, multigenerational hand-me-downs. I still didn't trust him; this was the longest conversation I'd ever had with him, or, for that matter, anyone in the Greek system. But I was willing to teach him how to be cool.

That afternoon, we met in the lobby and walked down the street to a cavernous vintage clothing store on Telegraph. He was a young man, I was an old one, and now we were sorting through secondhand polyester shirts, blazers of the deceased, dust everywhere as we shook open every new marvel. "I'm afraid to rub my eyes," he said, and I softened to him. I helped him pick out a shiny yellow shirt with ostentatious lapels. When he looked in the mirror, he affected a sad face, as though this shirt were leaching away his natural aura. It was perfect. Later, I went by his room to lend him a Playboy belt that I'd once bought as a joke in Taiwan. He wasn't around, so I left a note wishing him luck and telling him this belt would complete the look.

It turns out that Ken's frat was throwing a 1970s party, and his goal was to stand out by looking spectacularly garish. "It was perfect," he told me, as he returned my belt a few days later. He was still a little giddy. "We should hang out."

I had an ethnographer's curiosity about his epic nights out, those dispatches from a radically different front line. Instead of going to parties, I spent most Friday nights reading and listening to music. I'd sit in the third-floor lounge with a stack of CDs and some books about Marx or cultural theory, which seemed more intuitive to me than poetry. I wrote letters to friends who'd gone to school on the East Coast, wishing for classmates as cultured and refined as the ones they described. I cheerfully greeted everyone as they slumped out of the elevator, listening to their tales of missed encounters, wondering why drunkenness required people to articulate their level of drunkenness.

Ken noticed that I never really went out. More important, he noticed that I hoped to be noticed for this. I'd never touched alcohol, but it was mostly because I was a snob, not a straight-edge ideologue. I couldn't imagine letting down my inhibitions around people I'd be silently judging the whole time. I politely refused his invitations to his frat house, telling him that Greek life wasn't my "aesthetic," but I'd join him for a morning-after breakfast, instead.

Our dorm's third-floor lounge had a balcony with a couple deck chairs. It looked onto the roof of the dining hall. Sometimes, guys used it to cut hair. You weren't allowed to smoke on it, but people did anyway. One night, Ken saw me pretending to study and asked me to go out to the balcony for a smoke, even though neither of us actually smoked. He told me about the party he'd just come back from; I told him about Heidegger, making it sound as if I understood what I was talking about.

It became our code whenever we wanted to talk: *I need a smoke.* An escape from homework or a crowded room of strangers, it was all the same. We would meet on the balcony and talk about classes, or girls (I had little to contribute), or distant dreams. Leaning on the railing, chatting conspiratorially, pretending that we were smoking so that nobody would bother us. Occasionally, someone would come out and ask to bum a cigarette, and we would somehow make them feel dumb for thinking that's what we were doing. I would cough demonstratively if someone lit up. *Sorry, it's my asthma.*

At night, Paraag, Dave, and I lay in our bunks, arguing about inane, deeply important things, like whether Boyz II Men were better than the Beatles. Why our room, which was meant for three, was smaller than the doubles down the hall. Who had eaten the last of the samosas his father had dropped off at our dorm. If we would ever experience true love, and whether we would stay friends for the next four years. *Tommy Boy* versus *Billy Madison.* Was Ken Griffey Jr. the greatest ballplayer of our lifetime? Where did the weathered Bob Marley CD constantly playing in our room actually come from? Is *X-Files* actually going anywhere? Were video games a real sport? We spent so much of our time in this mode—sifting through culture as evidence, projecting different versions of ourselves based on our allegiances and enthusiasms. We weren't in search of answers. These weren't debates to be won: certainty was boring. We were in search of patterns that would bring the world into focus.

We craved new contexts, initiating routines that might eventually feel second nature. I'd introduced Alec, a nervy hippie across the hall, to the woeful beauty of the Kinks' "Waterloo Sunset." For a couple weeks, we convened in his room at the end of the day and listened to it reverently. Sometimes Irami and Ken joined us. Paraag heard about some guys on the fourth floor who took turns picking up the check for lunch. This seemed much more mature than how we'd been in high school, splitting everything five ways, shaking one another down for any debt greater than seventy-five cents. We wanted to be adultlike and magnanimous, too. We agreed to meet for a weekly, late-night dinner at Orchid, a Chinese restaurant a few blocks away from our dorm. It reminded me of family meals at home. But we were unaccustomed to ordering Chinese food for ourselves, the balance of dishes necessary for a proper, well-rounded feast. We kept it up for a few weeks, taking turns paying for the table, before concluding that the guys in Paraag's story had way more money than we did.

At first, Ken and I pretend-smoked because we were bored and shared a fondness for ritual; you repeat a gesture enough times until you're actually friends. One night, he brought a pack of cigarettes someone had left behind at a frat party. He smoked only when he drank, he said, lighting a cigarette. I never drank, so I figured only smoking was okay. I instantly liked it.

You repeat the ritual enough and you become actual smokers.

Smoking offers a way to build natural breaks into conversation. Lighting a cigarette starts a timer. We had to commence discussion of serious matters, accelerate the chitchat toward its most intimate intensities. Ken always looked very serious whenever he took a drag, eyes downcast, the cigarette hanging from his upper lip, bobbing up and down as he spoke. I loved practicing different ways of holding mine. Wedged between your index and your middle fingers, as if they were chopsticks. Pinched between your thumb and your pointer, as though you were about to squash a bug. Down by the knuckle, between your middle and your ring fingers, so that half your face was covered each time you drew a breath. Nestled in the curl of your forefinger, like a pool cue, so that you could use the lit end to gesture and point.

Ken and I swapped theories, looked for stories that might make our world seem more real. We talked a lot about television. We had been schooled to look for allegorical meaning, so of course we quested for alternative interpretations, unpacking all the tropes that governed our imaginations. We stretched our memories to come up with a list of every old TV show, every member of the 1984 San Diego Padres. There was no such thing as authority, just whoever could pull the randomest reference or narrate the most compelling take on some formative movie from our youth.

In those days, I fixated on the lamest things people did. I didn't trust anyone who tucked their shirts in. When Ken tried to get me to listen to classic rock—or, worse yet, Pearl Jam—I recoiled in disgust, as though he were presenting a virus. When he told me about his plan to move to Boston after graduation, I admired his vision—far beyond San Diego. But Boston was lame. I wanted to go to New York. When he started reading philosophy and theory, I delved into even more obscure philosophy and theory. He recommended a book on hegemony and socialism by Ernesto Laclau and Chantal Mouffe. I scoffed, as if he had just praised the Pearl Jam of post-Marxist thought—*Oh yeah, I've heard of them*—and then I committed their names to memory.

He often wanted to talk to me about girls, an area of knowledge where my understanding was largely conceptual. All I'd ever learned about romance in high school was that *Schindler's List* is a terrible idea for a first date. It was an aspect of life I was still figuring out. Meanwhile, Ken unironically used words like "libido."

We started studying together at cafés and, when the circumstances required, the library. Sometimes, we met for breakfast so he could tend to his hangover with steak, eggs, and a side of pancakes. His stories were bizarre and funny to me: the time he and his brothers messed with a rival frat by stealing all the knobs from their stove and oven; the time one of his heftier brothers got his hand stuck in a carton of Goldfish. When Ken's enthusiasm for staying up all night and debating the subversive subtexts of movies overwhelmed mine, I wondered whether I was really unique. Maybe the thing that made me uneasy was realizing that we weren't very different after all. He often prodded at the persona I had built for myself. Why did I insist on being so weird? What compelled me to always order the most unusual item on the menu? Wasn't it all a ploy to be noticed by others? Especially, he would say accusingly, "artsy, alternative" girls? And hadn't I briefly owned the first Pearl Jam album, too?

We went for late-night drives in the Volvo I'd inherited from my mom. I made tapes for these drives, noisy pop songs clattering through the door panels. One night, he pointed to a hill. "Let's go up there." We had no idea what road would lead there, so we just kept moving, approaching, expelled down a one-way street, doubling back. Eventually, we found its base, and we started climbing above the lights, until it was dark. We could see the entire East Bay. He was memorizing how we had done it so that he could make use of this knowledge at some point when he had his own car. "You should bring Sammi up here, Huascene." Sammi was an artsy, alternative girl who lived on the fifth floor. I wanted to be her friend because she wore this cool green golfing jacket. *Yeah, whatever, man,* I scoffed.

Ken believed that everything we did in life was to make girls like us. The way we dressed, the music we listened to, our sense of humor. Being a sensitive and politically engaged person, making zines and mixtapes. It all came down to getting laid. *No,* I protested with a showy nonchalance. *How can you be so crass? I don't do anything for attention.* What if nobody understood the references I was making? he asked. *That's such a gauche way of thinking about it,* I said. *Some people get me,* I continued, and Ken let me talk myself into a corner. *I'm just into what I'm into. I don't do it to be noticed . . . I mean, not by everyone. Like, it's different from how you are. Like, I honestly don't believe in physical attraction; it's all about someone's intellect . . .*

He just nodded. *Attraction is more than physical appearance,* I continued. *I think calling someone "hot" is reductive and dehumanizing.* The humane thing for Ken to do was to let me keep talking, because I'd eventually run out of straws to grasp at. I appreciated that he was too kind to put me out of my misery and point out my insecurities. Maybe this is what it meant to be known, this feeling of being exposed and transparent.

. . .

Ken gave us an off-campus address and instructions to come by around five. We were to keep going upstairs, following a ladder up toward the noise. Dave, Paraag, and I ended up on some-one's rooftop, where about twenty guys we didn't know were barbecuing unsuccessfully. Ken began introducing us to every-one. There were no girls, which was fine by me. A few of them casually encircled Dave; then, as though following some kind of choreography, others did the same to Paraag, then me, smoothly quizzing us about our hometown, prospective major, whether we had season tickets to Cal football.

I had no idea whose house this was. Sparks kept flying over the edge and onto the street below. I eventually extricated myself from a conversation with a fellow political science major whose name I instantly forgot. Soon, I found Ken, who was tending to the burgers. *Is it okay to be up here?*

"Who cares?" he said. "We are."

After a few more rounds of conversation, I realized that everyone I spoke to was a member of his fraternity, and they were assessing Dave, Paraag, and me as potential brothers. *Are you trying to . . . are we being pledged or rushed or whatever you call it?* I asked Ken quietly, half-offended, half-flattered. I liked him, and I even admired one of his brothers, Derrick, a cheerful, fatherly engineering major from our dorm. I briefly imagined being their brother. Ken blushed. "Yeah I just thought you were cool. Maybe you'd be into all this." He handed me a tiny burger, blackened and hard. "Grab a briquette, Huascene." We looked at this charred little piece of beef and laughed. "Don't worry about the guys. Just have fun."

In the late 1980s, the philosopher Jacques Derrida delivered a series of seminar lectures on the subject of friendship. He was, at that point, one of the most famous philosophers in the world, having become synonymous with the idea of deconstruction. Derrida wanted to disrupt our drive to generate meaning through dichotomies—speech versus writing, reason versus passion, masculinity versus femininity. These seeming opposites were mutually constitutive. Just because one concept prevailed over the other didn't mean that either was stable or self-defined; straightness exists only by continually marginalizing queerness, for instance. His methods required a closer examination of what was being lost or suppressed: in doing so, he and his acolytes argued, we would come to recognize that concepts that seem natural to us are full of contradictions. Perhaps accepting this messiness would lead us to a more conscious and intelligent way of living.

Derrida's lectures were published in 1994 in a book titled *The Politics of Friendship*, full of these dense, associative dives into the ideas of Aristotle, Nietzsche, Kant, and the political theorist Carl Schmitt. Each lecture returns to a line attributed to Aristotle, *o philoi, oudeis philos.* The line is often translated as "O my friends, there is no friend"—a strange sentiment, affirming yet negative. Some speculate that Aristotle was expressing something simpler, closer to "He who has many friends, has no friend." But Derrida was drawn to the seeming paradox of the translation he favored. By focusing on the tension inherent in the friend and the enemy, public and private life, the living and the "phantom," he imagined pointing us toward the possibility of new connections.

I knew a graduate student in Berkeley's Rhetoric Department who flew to Irvine each week to attend a seminar taught by Derrida. He'd come back to campus and tell me about how close he sat to the legend himself. There were rumors that one of the most important thinkers of the day loved Taco Bell. At the time, I had no idea Derrida was alive, let alone that he was spending the mid-1990s in places like Irvine. All I knew about Derrida was that he was important.

We wrestled with pared-down versions of all this in our classes, applying his overarching skepticism toward received wisdoms that informed our own world. Everything we learned cast doubt on our fixed ideas. Suddenly I started describing anything that was taken apart as being "deconstructed." Anything weird was merely "postmodern." Maybe, in fact, there was no truth. The word itself was meaningless. How did we come to agree on the meanings of words to begin with? Talking about all of this was fun. Multiculturalism, and the inclusion of women and minorities in the canon, still felt like a meaningful intervention. But what if your issue was with the very notion of standards and hierarchies? Critics of Derridean deconstruction worried where these questions might take us. We could seek nuance and refine our political positions forever. How would we dream together if we couldn't agree on any common values?

It was hard to unlearn the usefulness of dichotomies. They made the world so much cleaner. I had defined myself by what I rejected, and these choices often hardened into something that felt political. It was about your sense of the world and what you expected from it. Aligning with this band instead of that one. Reading zines rather than corporate media. I'd chosen the bookish sarcasm of Blur over their rivals, Oasis, whose fan base now seemed dominated by uncouth jocks. But then, I listened to their new albums during the first semester of college, and I determined that they were both dreadful. There were more choices than I initially realized.

One night, back when we were in the dorms, Ken appeared on our floor, almost theatrically breathless. Something had happened. He went from room to room. He needed our help. No girls. "I can explain on the way."

We followed him to a convenience store. He bought an armload of Snapples, handing each of us two bottles. Some rival frat had jumped one of his brothers. He was okay, he didn't get that hurt, but we would seek revenge anyway by smashing their windows. *Wait, what?* I protested. *Who is "we" here? "We" are not even part of your idiotic frat.* He slurred his way through a speech about loyalty, true brotherhood, plausible deniability. We were his brothers, even if we weren't officially so. We followed him up the hill anyway; nobody wanted to let him down.

We paired up and made our way up Bancroft. I drifted a few steps behind the pack. Ken casually sauntered up to the house and heaved his bottle at the front window. Before I heard the glass shatter, I was sprinting back to our rendezvous point in the Unit 1 quad. I ran as fast as I could, hearing sirens in the distance, wondering if we would get arrested, realizing that was stupid. I thought about all the terrible things happening somewhere else in Berkeley that night. Ken's brother was worth avenging because Ken was worth helping. I got to Unit 1 first and realized I was still holding my Snapples. I searched in vain for a recycling bin before dropping them in a trash can and waiting. Ken was the last to arrive. "I've never seen you run that fast," he said, laughing. "Huascene booked before the bottle was out of my hand." We returned to our dorm, where we were hailed as heroes.

The thing you learn in college is how to live with other people, and Ken understood this at an instinctive level. The next day, he bought us all hoagies, which we ate on the benches across Bancroft from the rival frat so we could snicker at the lone, boarded-up window. We might as well have won the Super Bowl. Ken knew how to use people—not in an exploitative way, but he understood what key you sang in. He could inspire you to do strange things, and he knew when to defer. Derrida remarked that friendship's driver isn't the pursuit of someone

who is just like you. A friend, he wrote, would "choose knowing rather than being known." I had always thought it was the
other way around.

Modern life, theorists like Derrida explain, is full of atom-
ized individuals, casting about for a center and questioning the
engine of their lives. His writing is famously intricate, full of
citations and abstruse terminology. Things are *always already*
happening. But reflecting on his own relationships tended to
give his thinking and writing a kind of desperate clarity. The
intimacy of friendship, he wrote, lies in the sensation of rec-
ognizing oneself in the eyes of another. We continue to know
our friend, even after they are no longer present to look back
at us. From that very first encounter, we are always preparing
for the eventuality that we might outlive them, or they us. We
are already imagining how we may someday remember them.
This isn't meant to be sad. To love friendship, he writes, "one
must love the future." Writing in the wake of his colleague Jean-
François Lyotard's death, Derrida wonders, "How to leave him
alone without abandoning him?" Maybe taking seriously the
ideas of our departed friends represents the ultimate expression
of friendship, signaling the possibility of a eulogy that doesn't
simply focus attention back on the survivor and their grief.

We were always being asked to read things for which we were
unprepared. How can Foucault possibly make sense mere days
into college? But you read anyway, confident that there would
come a day when you could pull from Adorno or Hegel. For
now, you underlined the parts that sounded as if they applied to
your life, your perspective, whittling these systems of thinking
down into something usable, like a sudden disdain for Nike. All
of this would make sense soon—maybe when we were juniors.

The present was a drag. We lived for the future. Youth is
a pursuit of this kind of small immortality. You want to leave

something behind. Record a single and put it out in the world, the part of the world that never dies, granted new life in the used bins and secondhand shops. Nestle your zines and manifestos inside newspapers around campus, between the pages of magazines left behind in cafés, your words against theirs. Spraypaint another's initials in the parking garage. You hurtle toward the future where you might look back upon the intricate secret handshake and laugh at how silly it once was, if you can remember it at all.

We sought a modest kind of infamy. Ken and I used to study at a particular table in the library, in the interstitial zone between where various Asian fraternities and sororities flirted with one another. They had a different kind of pride; they claimed AZN pride, and they were aliens to us. We would make each other keel over in laughter by miming lengthy, silent drum solos, sliding a bag of gummy bears back and forth, like some slow, erratic game of air hockey. Above us was a plaque with a painting of an old white man. Beneath him were the names of everyone who had earned whatever award was named in his honor. We would write our names on slips of paper and sneak them into empty spaces underneath him, wondering how long it would take before someone noticed us.

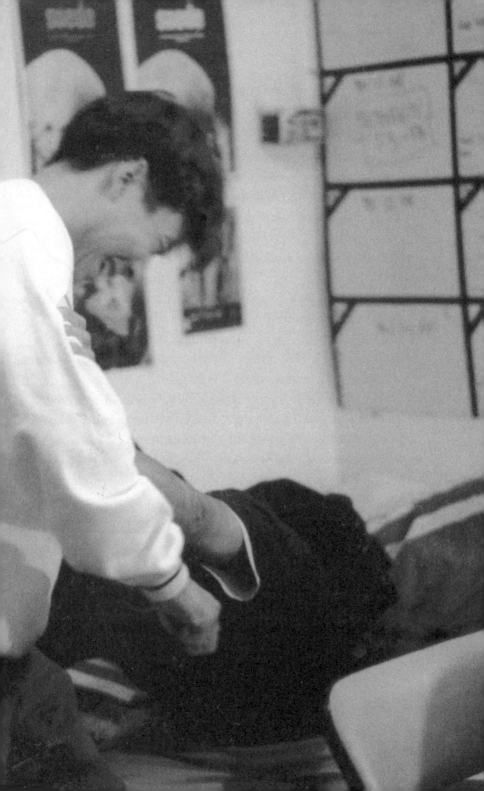

WE WERE ON THE ROOF of our dorm, just after dinner, waiting for the sunset. It was late May—the beginnings of T-shirt and shorts weather, though I opted for a striped, wool sweater I'd recently thrifted. Finding our way to the summit of Ida Sproul Hall was a final curiosity satisfied before moving out. Soon, we would be sophomores living off campus, dispersed throughout Berkeley, maybe Oakland. There were rumors of some juniors who lived all the way in San Francisco. We might need bikes, maybe even a car, to see one another. *Does the bus stop there?* We looped our cameras around our necks and took turns climbing up the service ladder.

The light felt rich with possibility. You wanted to believe there was no better time or place on earth than this, right now. It was a bunch of us from the third and fourth floors, as well as Anthony, who lived in a different dorm but never passed up the chance for adventure. We took pictures of one another, all these random group shots of not-quite-friends. We were now joined by this moment, since we would all be in trouble if anyone found us up here. From ten floors up, the clock tower looked close enough to reach out and touch, and the campus, which seemed vast and unknowable, came into view as a unified whole. The sun was setting. You realized how haphazard this place was, these lecture halls, offices, laboratories, meadows, and dormitories climbing a hill until they could go no farther.

I have a picture of Ken. His elbows rest on the ledge. He is looking up from his camera toward the San Francisco Bay. Maybe he looks past it, and maybe he is wondering where, in this wide-open space, he will land. I have a photo only of him looking, not what he is looking at.

He was always anticipating the future. A whisper during a movie trailer: "Let's go see that when it comes out." Someday, on the horizon, when we would master the campus's enormity. When his Cuban Sugar Kings baseball cap would be tastefully faded, worn in, the bill curved just right. When this spot on our couch would be his spot. Junior year, paths in view, pursuing our specialized passions. When we would come visit him in El Cajon and he'd take us to Barona. When he would be the wise, older brother that the fresh-faced frat initiates consulted for advice. Turning twenty-one, free to enjoy a casual Newcastle Brown Ale. Free to enjoy a Samuel Smith's Nut Brown Ale. Free to enjoy a Zima. Free to walk into a bar and enjoy whatever and however much he wanted. But first: a ceremonial round of birthday shots.

When the Padres would be good again. When that one Abercrombie jacket, the blue and red one, would be back in stock. When we'd have more money, and a dollop of sour cream on our burritos wouldn't seem excessive. When we would be seniors, researching our theses. When we would graduate— the real world awaited. When he would be in Boston, going to graduate school, slinging peanuts at Fenway Park. When we would be grown-ups reminiscing about being dumb teenagers.

Before all that, there was our next smoke. Pull the strip and peel back the cellophane. Smack it against your wrist. Flip the lucky one around. A fresh pack of cigarettes, twenty more conversations.

Paraag, Dave, and I survived the tininess of our triple—which, on the rarest of occasions, stretched to a quadruple—as friends.

We weathered the single, shared phone line, various petty scuffles, numerous disagreements about whose turn it was to vacuum, a mold scare, our private terrors about measuring up in a first-year class of around eight thousand students. None of this meant we wanted to continue living together. Paraag moved in with Sean; they found a place behind the Blockbuster on Channing. A high school acquaintance who was a year older than us invited Dave to take his spare room. As we packed up, that last day before move out, we were euphoric for our new beginnings. Henry from down the hall went room to room, documenting the afternoon with his camcorder. Bone Thugs-N-Harmony's "Tha Crossroads" spilled out from various stereos. I pretended to ignore him, before jumping in front of the video camera, belting out the "bone-bone-bone" part of the song, and then sprinting away.

Anthony and I moved into a two-bedroom bungalow on Dwight Way. Ken had come with us to check it out during finals week, hopeful that it might accommodate three people. After looking around for a few minutes, he decided to move into his frat house instead.

Our place was about five blocks from campus, which felt a brave distance. The fact that the previous tenants had left behind a couch, some racing tires, a disassembled drafting table, and some hip-hop 12-inches contributed to a sense that we were growing up. We now owned a couch. I could take up drafting, maybe become an architect, like Ken. We could soup up my Volvo and start street racing, if we wanted to.

I had met Anthony through Paraag and Dave, who often hung out with a group of friends who'd gone to Saratoga, one of our rival high schools. Anthony was a business major. One of the first things he put up in our apartment was a framed picture of piles of cash with the words "My First Million" underneath. I decorated my room with anti-corporate zines and flyers I'd picked up at the left-wing bookstore. Yet I appreciated Anthony's entrepreneurial streak. In high school, he had lived by himself in downtown Saratoga, so he clearly knew how to take care of himself. Freshman year at Berkeley, he found a job as a delivery boy for a coffee shop, and he funneled his earnings into a run of bootleg T-shirts he sold at Cal football games. I had no idea how he knew the racer-architect-DJs who used to live in our place, but it didn't surprise me. He was a hustler. Importantly, he also knew how to cook.

There was a built-in breakfast nook in the kitchen that looked as if it hadn't been cleaned since the 1980s. We threw a bedsheet over the couch and rested the tabletop on the tires for a coffee table. I absorbed the 12-inches into my record collection. I bought some small, triangular tables that looked cool but kept tipping over. I finally had enough space for my own stereo and turntable. Our porch looked onto Dwight. The first week there, I would sit outside with a canvas and some acrylics and attempt to paint.

Ken was back in El Cajon. He wrote me a letter telling me to check my email, because he was going to be using his dad's AOL address over the summer. I had missed a trip that some of our friends had taken down south after finals, and he recounted the highlights to me. It was good to be home, he wrote in the letter, but he looked forward to coming back up to Berkeley soon. He signed off with one of our inside jokes, one whose origin I can't recall: "Stay true, Ken."

Anthony and I celebrated the occasion of living in the farthest off-campus apartment of anyone we knew by throwing a party. I'd never thrown a party before; my preparation involved making a mixtape that was quickly tossed aside as soon as people arrived and wanted to listen to something non-depressing. Neither Anthony nor I drank, but everyone was free to bring vodka, beer, whatever. It was summertime, and a lot of our friends had remained in Berkeley to take electives or work retail. Ken drove up for the party. He brought us a housewarming gift: a set of glasses. It seemed so practical and grown-up. They're as much for me as for you, he explained, assuring us he'd frequently be over to use them. He also gave me a birthday present, since he'd be back home on the day. A wooden desk tray for addresses, phone numbers, and business cards. He told me it was for my zine so I could keep in touch with my readers. He pulled out one of the blank cards and wrote down his name and home address, filing it under *I*. "Keep in touch," he joked.

Soon, people would lose their relationship to something called free time. We would no longer be bored, for there was always something to do or buy, something new to look up and learn about, some conversation to crash. But, at the time, there was nothing better than a Friday with no plans, alone to tinker with my zine. The expansiveness of a free night, writing so that I might appear in my own lines, even if nobody would ever read them. A series of one-sided crusades, all these manifestos that circulated among a cadre of two or three. It was only in my zine that I admitted to dreaming of anything great. In real life, I feared stepping into too large a world and failing. But I wrote things that were earnest and open, that I would never dare say out loud.

Sammi was subletting a place around the corner for June and July. I tried to sound as deep as possible as I told her I was spending the summer painting and making a zine. Sammi was from New York, not Northern or Southern California, which qualified her as the coolest person I'd met thus far at Berkeley. She volunteered to work on the zine with me. I showed up each day at her apartment with a couple sandwiches and a bag of Doritos. We would listen to her Mojave 3 CD and work at her coffee table. I had never heard Mojave 3, but their songs were perfect, like witnessing something beautiful happening in slow motion. I aspired to move through the world this deliberately. Since I judged people by their CD collections, I held Sammi in very high esteem. I wrote endless, over-the-top reviews of obscure power-pop singles from Canada, mimicking the hyperactive styles I'd read elsewhere. Compared with Sammi's poems, which, by virtue of making no sense to me, struck me as deeply original, my contributions to the zine suddenly felt trite and obvious.

By sophomore year, I was officially a political science major, drawn to how easy it was to say very little in each class and still earn an A minus. I kept pace by listening to people who spoke a lot and wondering if I could have generated those insights, too. My classes were largely filled with gregarious, chummy white people from beach towns on their way to becoming lawyers, so the greatest challenge involved summoning the courage to raise my hand once or twice a semester so that I wouldn't fail the participation portion of our grade. I didn't want to be a lawyer, though I had trouble imagining alternate paths. I was quickly coming to the realization that my creative anxieties about whether there was anything original or new left to say about the world were quite generic. I couldn't get anything published by *The Daily Cal,* our school newspaper. I was probably not an artist. I was definitely a terrible painter. I was in search of a narrative engine, some kind of spark that might organize my surplus energies. Maybe, if I was lucky, I could channel my love of research into a job at a think tank.

I wanted to become fluent in philosophy and cultural theory, so I started taking courses in the Rhetoric Department. A rhetoric seminar I took during my first semester of college consisted in our reading Foucault with minimal oversight; I took the hands-off approach to be part of the department's radical pedagogical ethos. There was a rumor that rhetoric faculty were the only ones on campus who were free to smoke in their offices.

I had no idea what rhetoric was, only that it was a word I'd apparently been misusing all throughout high school. *That's just rhetoric,* I would say, whenever someone tried to pass off opinion as fact. The department's course offerings didn't abide by any obvious logic, spanning everything from Aristotle to television to structures of meaning, the nature of selfhood, the futility of language. A dictionary entry defined "rhetoric" as the art of persuasion. None of it made sense to me. Maybe I was right after all: everything is, literally, *just rhetoric.* This was very exciting to me.

Ken no longer wanted to become an architect. Now he wanted to go to law school, and the art of persuasion seemed a useful skill to hone, so he tried some rhetoric classes, too. I was glad to have an ally through these strange journeys, as well as someone to measure myself against. We took an intro course on language that focused on what it meant to "perform" a promise. I doodled pictures in Ken's notebook of our instructor, who straddled his lectern in an almost erotic fashion. We took an upper-division class on the philosophy of time. Each meeting sounded like a conversation you might have on drugs, or so I imagined. We read Heidegger and Wittgenstein, applying the bits we understood to science fiction stories, reveling in the infinite delights of forking time lines, paradoxes, and loops, the catastrophes that would ensue if two divergent paths met. Maybe there was a way out of these puzzles that nobody had thought of yet.

I was eager for a future that might take place anywhere else, a new scene where my awkwardness would be mistaken for nonchalance. School was easy and I was surrounded by people who liked or at least tolerated me. But I was stridently noncommittal to them. I always left myself an out, an escape hatch in case someone offered me a new adventure, the adventure I thought I deserved. I looked forward to a time when I would be the finished article, my sense of the world innate and effortless, with no evidence that there had been any rough drafts.

I have a photo that Anthony took that fall semester in the bungalow. He was always taking pictures, as if he had been designated to document our lives. It's October 1996. Paraag, Ken, and I are sitting on my bed under a massive dry-erase board calendar that spanned the entire wall. Sammi and I had made the calendar over the summer. I used it to keep track of my homework assignments, the amount of money I spent each day, the release dates of CDs and movies, random things other people said that I found funny ("Hua has a lot to say, but can't be bothered to say it"). Paraag has dropped by to say hi. He's hunched forward, elbows on his knees, smiling, as though he were testing out the most confidence-projecting angle. Ken is between us, and he leans toward me playfully. I've just gotten a haircut and I'm wearing my favorite Fred Perry shirt and carpenter jeans. I'm pressed against him, trying to make everyone laugh by crowding his private space. My eyes are closed; I pretend to lick his ear. Ken has a look of mock despondency. He stares directly at the camera with a bemused grin, as though he were the straight man suffering through a moment of slapstick.

Ken has come over to study, but I've just bought two CDs, one of which sits on the edge of my desk: *From the Muddy Banks of the Wishkah,* a collection of live Nirvana recordings. I had some concert bootlegs where it sounded as if someone had thrown a heavy blanket over Kurt Cobain's microphone. But these performances were urgent and crisp. I was amazed that there could be even more Nirvana in the world. I'd moved on from them at the apex of their fame. Now that they were no longer as popular as when I was in high school, I felt a nostalgic fondness for these songs.

The mystery of newly discovered, posthumous recordings suggested that you could discover something new about yourself, too. Cobain's songs described a stifling present—his present. It was strange to imagine that the anguish, which defined his reality, carried well into the future, beyond his life, so that we could share in it, adopt it as our own. It was tempting to read strain and struggle in every moment of this CD, signs of what was to come. After Cobain died, every detail of his life slotted into a narrative of rising and falling. Boredom, frustration, angst, loneliness, joy: it all became clear later, bundled together as the tempestuous life force that drove him, not just the unsettling textures that defined his daily life.

Ken liked Nirvana, too, just not while we were trying to study. He kept beckoning me back to our readings. I figured he was the type who probably got into them only after "Smells Like Teen Spirit" was a big hit. He preferred Pearl Jam. He'd once gone to great lengths to find a copy of one of their B sides, he proudly told me. It was a sign of personal growth, I thought to myself, that I could be friends with someone who liked Pearl Jam this much. Yet the more we hung out, the less certain I was of these distinctions. Ken was cool in a way that had nothing to do with mastering random, arcane fields of knowledge. He was comfortable with himself, whether this meant chatting up girls at frat parties or accompanying me to the record store, and passing back and forth seemed to require no effort on his part.

You make a world out of the things you buy. Everything you pick up is a potential gateway, a tiny, cosmetic change that might blossom into an entirely new you. A bold shirt around which you base a new personality, an angular coffee table that might reboot your whole environment, that one enormous novel that all the fashionable English majors carry around. You buy things to communicate affiliation to a small tribe, hopeful you'll encounter the only other person in line buying the same obscure thing as you. Maybe I, too, will become the kind of person who has books like *Infinite Jest* casually strewn on his cool, angular coffee table. Maybe I'll become the kind of person who seems as if he should have that book but chooses not to. I spent hours at Amoeba Music, walking back and forth in the same few sections ("Rock," "Indie"). There was an entire other wing devoted to jazz and something called world music; I looked forward to one day becoming the type of person who understood these genres and, by extension, the world. One day, I bought a jungle 12-inch based purely on a description I'd read in a magazine. At first, I thought the record was defective, since it was nothing but jittery drums and a bass line that kept making the needle skip. Where was the rest of the song? But then I realized it was supposed to sound this way, that this bass line was a portal to somewhere new, and I couldn't wait to hear more. I started picking up rave flyers at coffee shops and record stores. It was electrifying to think about how much more music there was in the world left to hear.

. Similarly, there's an intimacy to going shopping with someone else, letting yourself get dragged into stores you would otherwise avoid. I'd go with Ken to musk-scented menswear shops so he could buy a new jacket or baseball cap, and in return he'd come with me to Cody's, the bookstore across from Amoeba that had the biggest selection of magazines I'd ever seen in my life. I always took much longer than he did at his stores. He patiently browsed sections that didn't interest me ("Men's Lifestyle") while I looked for new zines, independent comics, European music magazines. One day, he bought a couple titles I'd never heard of. One was the first issue of *Maxim,* which seemed cartoonishly horny, full of swimsuit models and gadgets. He assured me that the articles were far cleverer than you would think. The other was a small, local magazine called *Might*. He was drawn to the provocative cover question, "Are Black People Cooler Than White People?"

Eventually, Ken asked to write for my zine. He would sometimes do his homework while I carefully annotated my anti-consumerist riffs or wrote reviews of other, larger zines that I admired. I grilled him as though deciding whether to give him his big break. Our tastes were so different. I'd never consider publishing any of his thoughts on music, so he wrote me a short essay about Wally Joyner, a star who had just joined his beloved San Diego Padres for the 1996 season. He printed it out and handed it to me. *This doesn't really fit what I'm trying to do. And my readers are quite cosmopolitan . . . they don't really care about . . . baseball.* He took my criticism with aplomb. He edited it into a self-consciously cliché-riddled op-ed about sports fandom, underdogs, and the hypocrisies of the team I'd loved as a child, the San Francisco Giants. I told him I'd try to publish it in a future issue, and I filed it away.

I started subscribing to various email listservs devoted to indie music. Email was no longer a dumb, bureaucratic encumbrance. It was now a reason to rush home after class. I studied the recommendations and references of the listserv messages more closely than my course readings. Email was like discovering a new genre for writing, one with its own, unique registers of wit and intimacy. Someone on the listserv lived on Fulton Street, just around the corner from me. He invited me over one night and played me some records by his friends. It felt cool to know someone who knew people in a band. But I felt more at ease emailing with him. I wrote long, soul-baring messages to other list members from Chicago or Halifax or Madrid whom I never imagined meeting. I traded mixtapes and zines with people who, by virtue of not having email addresses that ended with .edu, seemed sophisticated.

I felt a little bad excluding Ken from this world I was discovering. He told me he wanted to meet people who knew people in bands, too. But I figured there was little I could do to truly shake his confidence. He saw people as innately good and open-minded. I saw a bad CD collection as evidence of moral weakness. This part of me never rubbed off on him. Instead, he took my gentle ridicule and asked for me to tape him Mojave 3 and Push Kings songs. I later wondered what he got out of my zine. Whenever he expressed skepticism toward the status quo, I felt a tiny measure of victory—*Join me on the side of cynical despair!* Maybe it was my influence, with the red star I'd cut out of felt and pinned to my jacket, telling anyone who asked that I was a Marxist.

One day, toward the middle of the semester, our professor showed us *La Jetée,* a short film by the French filmmaker Chris Marker. It was a simple tale of a future civilization trying to time travel their way out of doom. We felt the rush of trying to grasp something lofty and difficult, grafting our basic understanding of physics to our even more basic understanding of Heidegger. I was captivated by Marker's ability to do so much with so little. The film mainly consists of a series of still black-and-white images with minimal voice-over. I believed that I appreciated his resourcefulness on a deeper level; it reminded me of a zine. I thought I could make a killer short film of stills and voice-over, too, if only I could come up with a good story.

I rented a VHS copy of *La Jetée* and brought it back to my bungalow so I could study it on my own. Ken liked it, too, and said to tell him when I was going to rewatch it. I distinguished myself by the ferociousness of my attachments; there was something unique about my fascination with the film, something Ken couldn't possibly understand. I was proprietary about liking things. I bought the assigned Heidegger pamphlet, where he had simply photocopied mine. We both liked *The Thin Blue Line,* another film that the professor had screened for us; only I went so far as to buy the soundtrack to listen to while driving. I wanted to claim Marker as my own. I offered him an overly vague window for when I planned to watch it again. But I was being dumb. Ken came over so often, and the rental lasted only seven days, it made no sense to incur late fees just to watch it alone.

We were captivated anew. *La Jetée* runs twenty-eight minutes long, so it wasn't difficult to rewind and repeatedly rewatch it, talking through its paradoxes and possibilities. Despite the low-grade urge to maintain my sense of eclecticism, I enjoyed sharing that feeling of total awe with Ken.

La Jetée takes place after World War III. Humanity's only survivors live underground. Scientists have figured out a way to send someone backward or forward through time, only most travelers go mad in the process. They eventually find a prisoner mentally strong enough for this mission "to call past and future to the rescue of the present." He is haunted by a prewar memory from his childhood. It returns to him in flashes: a beautiful woman waiting at the airport, a man dying just short of her arms. They are fragments of a story he feels but can't tell.

But the power of this memory seems to draw him through time, offering him a kind of resiliency that other travelers lack. He doesn't realize that this memory is a warning—that he is the one who dies, because those in power will have no use for him once he saves the world. He's caught in a loop, and whatever is fated to happen will happen. We watched it and then watched it again; each time, his world ends.

.   .   .

Ken taught himself to light a match with one hand, curling one out of the book and flicking it aflame. I practiced until I could do it, too. We became proper smokers, delighting in the ritualism of it all. One time, during a cigarette break from studying, he told a story about seeing his ex-girlfriend. They had once been sweethearts in high school, but after a few semesters of college that was an entire consciousness ago. They were sitting on the dock of a lake house, their toes skimming the water. She felt the sun to be radiant and generous, and she wanted to bask in it. "My life has always been a dream," she said to him. She was popular, kind, and pretty; she was comfortable but never spoiled. Not that any of that was the problem. After all, he had once loved her, loved all the goodness that she embodied. It was something else. "Can you believe she said that?" Ken said to me.

I didn't follow. *Are you still into her? Do you want to get back together with her?*

No, that's not it, he said with a sigh. Now he seemed disappointed in me, too.

He took a drag from his cigarette. "My life has always been a dream," he repeated. "A dream." He was mystified that she thought he could relate to this feeling. "My life has never been *a dream.*"

Friendship is about the willingness to know, rather than be known. Ken sometimes tried on my old, disintegrating cardigans or thick, polyester shirts, an attempt to understand why I looked like a hobo. It was his way of reckoning with what I saw, why I stood the way I did. Hearing about his disillusionment disturbed my sense of who he was. I delighted in being the playful cynic, comfortable in a constant state of not belonging. He was the least cynical person I knew, to the point where I assumed his life had, indeed, been a dream. I thought about making a joke about the hazards of falling in love with white people but decided to leave him there, wherever he was. I realized how wrong I'd been to assume that his life was a breeze, shot through with invincible golden hues. I even felt protective of him in that moment, surprised, and slightly awed, by the fact that he held on to such grand visions of what life could offer.

I remember the first time I saw Jesse Jackson speaking on the steps of Sproul Plaza, during our freshman year, demanding that we arise in defense of affirmative action. It felt remarkable to stand so close to a hero and to be called by him into history. A few weeks later, he was back, propelled by some other cause, and then there he was again, a few months later, reminding us to stand up and be counted. It seemed that Jesse Jackson was always on campus.

We were part of something. In November 1996, Californians voted on Proposition 209, which sought to eliminate affirmative action from school admissions and government contracts. That semester, I'd gotten a job at the campus tutoring center, where I worked with fellow undergrads who needed help with their written work. I first came to admire our campus's diversity while sitting at my drop-in desk, watching the future business leaders and engineers alongside the football players and first-generation students from Oakland who'd grown up in Berkeley's shadow. Some of us were here for talents that were legible and bold, others were here for their potential, and we all had a lot to teach one another.

I marched in the streets as soon as it became clear that Prop

209 would be passed. That evening, I went to the campus clock tower. Some student protesters had chained themselves to the railing at the summit, refusing to come down until the legislation was overturned. A woman ran up the hill to tell us that Mario Savio, the famous free speech activist from the 1960s, had just died. The passage of Prop 209 must have been too much for him to bear, we thought. Someone grabbed a megaphone and began reciting his speech about throwing ourselves on the apparatus, putting our bodies on the levers of the machine, so that this whole odious system would cease to work. I wondered how many more people needed to show up for this to happen.

I followed the crowd wherever it took me. At times, it was as if the 1960s had never ended. There were reminders everywhere. I read every book I could find about the Black Panthers, and then I'd see them around Berkeley or Oakland, old men still wearing their movement-era leather trenches as if they were varsity football jackets from the glory days. I put a picture of the sprinters John Carlos and Tommie Smith raising their fists at the 1968 Olympics on my wall. Then I realized that my sociology professor had been in Mexico City with them. He had given them the idea to do it.

I started hanging out at the Ethnic Studies Library to read 1960s movement newspapers and photocopy images for my zine. I would photocopy photocopies of old protest leaflets until they were abstract, washed out, and blurry. The zine no longer existed as a way to scam free CDs from people; I now saw it as part of this broader political ethos of self-determination and free expression.

I was at the Ashby flea market one weekend when I met an older man named Melvin selling Black Panther memorabilia— color reproductions of old posters, pins featuring Huey Newton and Bobby Hutton, cassettes of speeches. I bought a Stokely Carmichael tape and a pin of Fred Hampton. Melvin was dressed like the men in the photos he was selling. He joined the Panthers as a young man in the 1960s, and he still published a newspaper called the *Commemorator*. I volunteered to help, if he needed any.

A couple weeks later, on a rainy Saturday morning, I drove to the Commemoration Committee of the Black Panther Party's small storefront in Oakland. I was greeted by Melvin and another man. They were both wearing leather jackets, and they weren't quite sure what to make of my eagerness to help. They handed me a Styrofoam cup of coffee.

The other man had originally been part of the Seattle chapter. I asked if he'd been present for a famous shoot-out I had read about, or whether he crossed paths with Leonard Peltier, the indigenous activist who'd been active in the Pacific Northwest. He paused for a moment to sip his coffee and weigh in his mind whether it would be more efficient to humor me or let me down. "Yes," he said, looking into his cup. "I remember him."

Melvin pointed me to their computer. They needed help formatting some of their articles. The next issue, he explained, featured a big story about a mysterious lynching in Anderson, a small town in Northern California. The body of a thirtysomething Black man was found hanging from a tree. I spent the rest of the day copyediting articles, adjusting captions, and making sure that the page jumps went to the right place. A black-and-white photo of the victim's mutilated body was on the cover. Fidgeting with typefaces and borders seemed like such a trivial set of tasks in the face of such horrors. When I finished, Melvin returned to the office and thanked me. I left my address so he could mail me some issues. He told me to give the extras to my classmates. It was 1997, Melvin said, and the Klan was resurfacing. He wasn't scared or paranoid, just resigned. They had never gone away.

What was it actually like back in the 1960s? Our proximity

to this storied time somehow made it seem even more impossible. All around us were people who had survived the events depicted in *Berkeley in the Sixties,* the documentary about the school's proud tradition of protest that screened during orientation week. Some were still wandering campus, dressed in sandwich boards, reciting manifestos at nobody in particular. Others had stuck around and become professors, disappointed that our generation splintered into various niche causes, pouring our energies into things that were small and meaningless. They had stopped a war.

There was an Iranian American kid our year who had started an ungraded, student-led class on the late Tupac Shakur. One day, during a lecture on medieval literature, he began thinking about the recently slain rapper and how hip-hop offered a way for people our age to rethink notions of heroism and chivalry. He came up with lesson plans and a reading list, considering everything from Afeni Shakur's days in the Black Panthers to the mainstreaming of hip-hop in the 1990s. This class was a serious endeavor, and reporters came from all over the country to gawk at the fact that you could now learn about rap music in college.

It was exciting to think that any one of us could contribute something audacious and weird to the course catalog. Was this the world that our predecessors had fought for? Was a diverse campus a sign of success or evidence that we could all join into the same, boring, bourgeois trajectory? Was Pac destabilizing our notion of a core curriculum, or was he now simply welcomed as an American outlaw, more proof of the nation's wicked capacity to make room for all?

Ken told me about an upper-division rhetoric seminar he was taking where the conversation turned to race. People began attacking one another, drawing a line in the sand between Black and white. It was as if he were describing some dramatic bar brawl. "This white chick started crying," he said, and then more people started crying. It was unclear where he stood in this conversation, if anyone noticed him to begin with. Quotations about complicity, victimhood, and color-blind racism were lobbed across the room, accusations flew inches from his face, and he was in the middle of it, neither Black nor white, scrutinizing the gestures and details that nobody else picked up on. He didn't cry. He was hardly seen at all. As he recounted the different characters, he was both energized and confused.

We were both Asian, conscious of all the stereotypes about being low maintenance and good at school. Yet we had come from such different worlds. I remember how odd it was that he sometimes forgot to take his shoes off when he came over. Growing up, Japanese Americans suggested a strange model of who all of us newer immigrants might become, a stepping-stone, generations into the future, toward some effortless sense of belonging. I attended a gripping lecture about Japanese internment during World War II and told him about it. He had family members who had grown up in the camps, he said, recalling some passed-down story about the children not realizing how bad things were since they got to play sports all day. I was in awe—and slightly envious—that he could draw such a legible connection to the history we learned in textbooks.

I thought this explained why we were so different. He felt some claim to American culture that I couldn't imagine. He joked about how different his life would have been with a name like Hiroshi Yamasaki, not the easy, mainstream Ken. I had no problem toiling away in the margins, mapping out a smaller world inside the larger one. Dreams of becoming a proper, widely read writer were dashed during my first year, when my submissions to *The Daily Cal,* our campus paper, were ignored.

Early during sophomore year, I came upon a flyer for *Slant,* a long-standing campus Asian American newspaper that a couple seniors were trying to relaunch. I finessed a semester's experience with *Slant* into an internship at a community newspaper in Chinatown, where I wrote about film festivals, art exhibitions, and local theater performances. Working for a newspaper that normal people had actually heard of seemed impossible. But I was unbothered, happy to paint myself into a corner, so long as it was mine.

For a while, I thought Ken bore a striking resemblance to Henry Cho, a Korean American comedian I'd seen doing stand-up on cable. Cho had an easy, accommodating smile and a singsong drawl. His shtick was that he was an observational comic and that these observations came from an Asian man in the South. Cheerful, self-effacing replies to casual racism. I brought home a promotional glossy of Cho from my internship and held it up against Ken's face. Cho wasn't very talented or funny, so Ken assumed I was dissing him. At least you look a bit like someone semi-famous, I explained, someone who's on TV.

One day, a casting agent for *The Real World* came to Ken's fraternity house, looking for prospective participants for the reality show. They often scouted the Greek system this way, setting up informal hangouts at campuses across the country and then offering formal auditions to anyone who seemed interesting. Ken was curious and checked it out. I was certain he would be chosen. I even began fantasizing about how I could turn his TV stardom into material for my zine. But if he was hoping to be discovered, he never would have admitted it to me.

Everyone was in the living room, trying their best to exude a mysterious yet accessible air for the people from MTV. Instead, Ken asked the casting agent why they had never had an Asian American guy on the show. *The Real World* had gone out of its way to represent various identities and personality types. What about us? "She told me we don't have the personalities for it," he said to me.

I started mocking the show as well as anyone who would ever try to be on it. I never thought to look for myself at the movies or on TV. We were too cool for that shit anyway. It was the principle, he explained. Our generation was more enlightened and tolerant and colorful than any that had come before. We had seen walls come tumbling down. And yet there was no room for people like us in this powerful casting agent's version of reality?

Ken wanted to see himself in the world. It was as though he were just now discovering that such a thing might not happen. "I am a man without a culture," he said, and I was surprised at both the dramatic tone of the sentiment and the fact that he already saw himself as a man.

We spent a lot of time in those days talking about sitcoms, trying to remember all the weird ones that lasted just a season, identifying all the tropes or character types that had made TV so pleasingly predictable. Short lists of all the times we remembered seeing an Asian delivery boy, maybe even a tertiary Asian acquaintance orbiting the main friend group. I thought we were just goofing off and passing time. But Ken was piecing together a theory about the world.

What does it mean to truly be yourself? Around this time, in the mid-1990s, the Canadian philosopher Charles Taylor began thinking about how people throughout history had dealt with this question of individual identity. In the past, there was no such thing. You were born into a well-defined position, locked along a hierarchy, and you accepted that this was the natural order of things. With the dissolution of feudal, old-world bonds, new possibilities of economic and social mobility emerged, and this transience infected the soul. People began to wonder whether we possessed some innate essence that might be discovered by peeling away layers of our surface. Or maybe there was nothing innate, and we were always in the process of self-discovery, self-creation, and revision. For some, this manifested as a kind of endless drifting and searching; others found the possibility of claiming one's own identity empowering. But we were all in search of the same thing, that quality that made you yourself.

Taylor called this authenticity, and it became the unreachable horizon of modern life. It's a concept that makes sense only in its absence; we recognize inauthenticity, phoniness, when someone's clearly being a poseur. Yet the struggle to feel authentic—this is very real, even if we know better. In Taylor's telling, everyone becomes a kind of artist, creatively wrestling with the parameters of our own being. He described the outlook as one where "being true to myself is being true to my own originality, and that is something that only I can articulate and discover. In articulating it, I am defining it." Even though all this sounds very navel-gazing, being true to yourself cannot happen in a vacuum. Constructing your personality is a game, one that requires you to joust with the expectations of others. Authenticity, Taylor explained, presumes dialogue, and it is born out of engaging with those around us. We seek recognition, even if what you want to hear from a close friend is that you're a one-of-a-kind weirdo that they'll never truly understand.

That winter, I pulled an all-nighter to finish the fifth issue of my zine. There was a page listing my favorite websites ("terrific Karl Marx site," "live Pavement recordings, all RealAudio"), stories from the Oakland warehouse raves where I'd go and dance by myself, dispatches from an Asian American film festival I'd covered for my newspaper internship, a poem by a beautiful skater girl I'd met through Anthony. I was sad when I received her poem and it was about a guy she liked, who was clearly not me. Consequently: reviews of many twee 7-inch singles that touted shyness as a virtue. A two-page spread of my favorite places to skateboard on campus, a list of my seven favorite 1980s Hong Kong films.

"Zines are a metaphor for life," I wrote in the welcome note. "It's your creation and your voice and your life . . . a form of expression that can be perverted by nobody and accepted/hated by everybody . . . Create, destroy, and subvert. Nobody will care about what you didn't say, if that makes sense. So go out there and shoot a video, make some racket, xerox a zine, and make your own indelible mark on the world." I left them tucked into magazines and newspapers at Wall Berlin or Milano. I had finally persuaded the buyer at Cody's to stock a few on consignment. I gifted a copy to a clerk at the elitist record store on University, and a week later I saw that he'd put it out for sale. I was flattered that he thought anyone would pay for it.

There was an organization on campus that seemed way too fervent about their defense of affirmative action. It was unclear if any of them actually went to Berkeley. One time, they were incensed at a column in *The Daily Cal* that had criticized them, and they held a rally next to a kiosk where stacks of the free newspaper were distributed. A man with a megaphone yelled, "I want you to walk over, and grab a stack of fascist *Daily Cals*, and dump 'em in that fountain!" A fellow protester whispered something to him. "Oh yeah, that's right. I want you to grab a stack of *Daily Cals* and RECYCLE THEM." The rumor was that this organization was funded by the CIA to discredit the rest of the campus's activists.

Ken and I were walking to class one day, when we came upon one of their demonstrations at Sather Gate. We both found their protest depressing, albeit for different reasons. I had started tutoring at an after-school program in Oakland, which brought me into this world of campus activists. I inherited their distrust of this organization and their over-the-top rhetoric. For Ken, it was more about pragmatism. He prized solutions that were strategic; maybe we could fight this in the courts. "What do you hope to accomplish with this protest?" he asked a huddle of organizers. "To make people aware of our plight," a woman explained, handing us a flyer. I wasn't sure what this meant, since she was white and not an obvious target of the right-wing effort to resegregate society. She and her comrades were blocking the gate. Next to her, there was an open passageway to campus and, above it, a sign meant to shame anyone who continued on their way: "White Males Only."

We weren't white males; we knew that. We just didn't know how to explain who we were, not in the space of a protest poster. Ken proposed that we write an op-ed together for the school paper. I wove some sarcastic jokes around his earnest, reform-minded questions. This movement needed barricades and grassroots organizers as much as it needed classrooms, legal challenges, people working for gradual change from within the system. Ripping allies who were simply trying to go to class seemed dumb and alienating—all the more so when we weren't actually white males. We ended our article with a note of smug glee, satisfied that we had exposed their small-mindedness.

Within a few months, I would understand that being in public, shouting, chanting, singing, calling out evil—it wasn't always about trying to accomplish something. Sometimes it's just about your voice blending in with those of others. The anonymity of being in a crowd, knowing you are there for one another. More feelings than you know what to do with, so you scream at someone, even if they're the wrong ones.

But, in the moment, we weren't sure what to do, so we just walked through the gate.

K EN AND I were studying in the library, underneath our plaque. I asked if he wanted to go have a smoke.

I loved walking with him. A mismatched pair moving through the world. We noticed the same things, taking in the small moments of everyday beauty and weirdness, like the distinctive, guttural way the man at the pizza place yelled, "Hot! Cheese! Pizza!" at passersby. It became a part of our everyday speech, a signal that it was time to eat. Maybe we'd run into someone, and Ken's dashing confidence would verify to this other person that I, too, was dashing and confident in my own, subcultural way.

When we finished our cigarettes, we were already on Telegraph. I asked if he would come with me to Amoeba for a few minutes.

A record store has a different energy after dark. It's filled with people who've wandered into the night in search of something. Ken trailed behind as I went from aisle to aisle. I showed him a box set featuring the complete recording sessions for the Beach Boys' *Pet Sounds,* an album I'd recently gotten into. My parents didn't have any of their records when I was growing up, which I took to be an informed judgment. But I sought out *Pet Sounds* after reading an article about the maniacal perfectionism that went into "God Only Knows," one of their most famous songs. It turned out the Beach Boys were pretty good.

Everything about the group was inauthentic: only one of them actually surfed, they were more indoor than outdoor kids, and whatever good vibes they conjured were incidental. Their breezy harmonies were less a reflection of collaboration and friendship than the bandleader Brian Wilson's micromanagement. He became so obsessed with translating his psychedelic visions into sound that it pushed him to the edge of reason.

I pointed to the seven different versions of "God Only Knows," a song that had become a key part of our world. *Is this ridiculous?* I wondered aloud. "You need this," he said, knowing it was what I wanted to hear. "Seven versions!"

When it was time to record "God Only Knows" in 1966, Brian asked his brother Carl to sing it. There was something about Carl's purity and tenderness that the authoritarian genius Brian lacked. Carl sings his heart out, constantly on the verge of breaking, only the song's steady, coasting rhythm carries him through. I had assumed that 1960s-style liberation was wild and frenzied. Here the harmonies had an almost cultlike intensity.

Ken and I returned to the library. I packed up my stuff and rushed home to listen to my new CDs. There was a version of "God Only Knows" that featured a brazen sax solo. One version that was strictly vocals, another that stripped it down to the backing harmonies, yet another that highlighted the strings. It was underwhelming hearing the song deconstructed into these parts. Not because they sounded slight and puny, but because I'd listened to the original so many times that it accrued a specific aura. "God Only Knows" suggested the possibility of yearnings beyond love. I couldn't locate these feelings in the song itself. Was it in the lyrics, these sad lines about drifting apart and rediscovering one's purpose? Was it in that magical vibration of voices intermingling, the fact that Carl conjured sensations Brian could write but never channel for himself? Maybe it wasn't in the song so much as in the repeated listenings, these memories stacking on top of one another.

.   .

By junior year, Anthony and I had moved into a condo on Channing Way. Paraag already lived there with Sean, a cocky Indian kid majoring in economics. Sean had a vanity license plate that read "BUCKWILD" and, despite being from Chino, a relatively quiet suburb in the San Bernardino Valley, claimed partial identity as a New Yorker, owing to a brief spell when he lived in New Jersey as a child. Sean was always mouthing off and nearly starting fights, introducing a lovably chaotic energy to our circle.

Our new place was just three blocks west, but suddenly we lived close to a cluster of our friends: Paraag and Sean were down the hall; Gwen lived up the street, on the corner of Channing and Fulton; a block away from her, Alec and Sammi shared a narrow two-bedroom apartment that wrapped around the back of a gas station.

Our Channing place had only one bedroom, so Anthony frequently spent the night at his girlfriend Wendy's. I aggressively decorated the entire place with gig flyers, Xeroxes from 1960s newspapers, and posters and banners from protests. My desk—a door propped up on two filing cabinets—took up an entire wall of our living room. I now had room not just for a stereo and my record collection but for a scanner, which I used for my zine. Now, instead of testing the limits of copy machines, I could manipulate images on my computer. Maybe I could become a graphic designer when I grew up.

This time, Ken's housewarming gift was a modernist clock with no numbers, just a white circle with the minute and hour hands poking out. I was an absolute baby about presents that I found insufficiently thoughtful. One year, a bunch of friends pooled together to get me a pager, even though I was clearly the type of person who resisted things like pagers. It was a constant reminder of how misunderstood I felt, each month, as I paid my pager bill. Ken felt the clock suited my style. It was cool in a way that felt aspirational and grown-up, and I adored it.

Ken moved out of the frat house that year, too. He lived with a couple friends on College Avenue, in a totally different part of Berkeley. *Is this even Berkeley? Is this the nice part of Oakland?* I had to drive to get there. We would walk down College to study at Roma, full of Berkeley students I'd never seen before, or eat at a Japanese restaurant, occasionally splurging for an appetizer. Then we would return and sit on his balcony, shaded by trees, and smoke our cigarettes. He began buying Nat Shermans and then, after seeing them in a movie, Export As. One of his roommates, who was white, had a fondness for off-color jokes about Asians, which Ken recounted to me with a pained weariness. He seemed older now. Maybe it was time to leave the frat, he thought aloud, or at least focus on his studies these last two years. In a certain light, at certain times of evening, his hair looked silver. It had once been long and wavy, caramel, and now he would occasionally buzz it short.

He asked if I wanted to start a club with him. The Multicultural Student Alliance would be a brotherhood of sorts. An ethnic studies professor had given an inspiring talk about how the movements of the 1960s had taught him what it meant to be a Chicano man. Ken intended to ask people like the professor to mentor us, teach us about our respective histories, share their experiences from when they were our age, maybe connect us with internships or jobs. It made sense to start thinking about the future now that we were juniors. I told him it sounded too much like his frat. We should be fighting for something more radical than multiculturalist inclusion, I said. Why not devote ourselves to tearing the whole rotten system down? Otherwise, this was just networking, and was this really why the professor had fought so hard back in the day? We were wasting our time, and his, too. Ken was irritated but undeterred. He thought a lot of people could benefit from something like this. He went ahead and got some buttons made, setting up a table on Sproul Plaza with someone I didn't recognize.

I had grown bored with my political science classes, all the discussions about disarmament, American litigiousness, the ins and outs of lobbying. I took as many ethnic studies and Asian American studies classes as I could, immersing myself in the traditions that had preceded us. It gave me solace to root around in the past and wonder if some of these moments of solidarity and action could find new spark with our generation. Out of principle, I stopped reading fiction. I wanted to learn only about histories that had been denied to us.

I volunteered at the Richmond Youth Project, a community center that worked with predominantly Southeast Asian middle school kids. I wasn't entirely clear on how one embarked on a career in research, or graphic design, so I thought teaching was a sensible backup plan. RYP was in a largely deserted shopping center right off the freeway. The few occupied storefronts catered to what the city, once a shipyard boomtown, had now become: a small church with an arcade out front; a fake hair emporium; a lonely military recruiter; graffiti in three or four different languages.

Every Friday afternoon, the Berkeley volunteers met near the Eucalyptus Grove, on a part of campus that I never knew existed. It was humbling to realize how much of the university remained a mystery, even as we lay claim to it as a place that was ours in these special and singular ways. We waited for people with cars to pick us up and drive to Richmond. I was apprehensive about driving somewhere so unfamiliar. It was about twenty minutes north, and on the way there we got to know one another—hometowns, majors, thoughts on mainstream versus underground hip-hop. I decided I needed to start listening to more underground hip-hop.

Everyone was Asian American; they looked like people I might already know, only their parents were bus drivers or restaurant workers, 1970s activists or leftist pastors, not engineers. I envied how at ease they felt whenever we went to Richmond. There were a few women from Oakland who were the first in their families to go to college; they'd been in programs like this when they were younger. In contrast, my trajectory was predictable, uninteresting. In those first few weeks, I never rode shotgun. I just sat in the back and listened.

We were twenty-year-olds teaching teenagers how to live for the future. There wasn't any real structure to the afternoon, other than hanging out, talking about what was going on in the lives of our mentees, doing homework together. Most of them were Mien. The Mien were originally an ethnic minority with roots in China. Between the seventeenth and the nineteenth centuries, fleeing persecution from the Han majority, they slowly resettled throughout Southeast Asia. They found a home in the highlands of Laos, where they subsisted as farmers, largely keeping to themselves. In the 1960s, as the Vietnam War tore through the region, the Americans enlisted the Mien to help beat back the Vietcong. Men with little grasp of modern technology were given machine guns. Two million tons of bombs were dropped on Laos, destroying the forests that the Mien relied upon and poisoning their water supply. After the Americans left, the surviving Mien took refuge in Thailand, and then the United States. Between 1976 and 1995, approximately forty thousand Mien refugees resettled in the United States. They found their way to places like Richmond, close to low-skilled jobs and affordable housing.

Our students had a vague sense of all this, thanks in part to their families and the center. I knew this history because of an Asian American studies class I was taking on the Southeast Asian diaspora. There were aspects of their lives that felt familiar. Their parents were busy working as many jobs as they could, and whatever connection they maintained to the past had more to do with household tradition than politics. Words like "genocide" and "trauma" were forbidden.

After a while, I started driving to Richmond, too. I worked mostly with the seventh-grade boys, who seemed to share a wardrobe, swapping their aggressively baggy, hand-me-down jeans, Nike sweatshirts, and windbreakers. A FUBU jersey for special occasions. Hair was shaved tight on the side, with wispy bangs parted in the middle, so their heads were always cocked a tiny bit forward. I thought being present and patient was enough, because I didn't have much perspective on the particulars of their lives. The fact that we were all Asian mattered more to me than my mentees. To me, Asian American was a messy, arbitrary category, but one that was produced by a collective struggle. It was a category capacious enough for all of our hopes and energies. There were similarities that cut across nationality and class: the uncommunicative parents, the cultural significance of food, the fact that we all took our shoes off at home. Our young mentees just had to realize such a community was for them, too.

Their worldviews were shot through with an everyday tribalism. There was such a thing as Asian pride. But even this meant you were Mien, Hmong, maybe Laotian or Vietnamese. As a Taiwanese American whose parents came decades earlier for grad school, I might as well have been from Mars. The boys borrowed a lot from their Black classmates, and they probably had more in common with them than with people like me. One afternoon, I was driving a few of them home, when some teens in the next lane looked over and scowled. They weren't Mien. One of my students flashed a pistol—which I didn't know he had—and the other car peeled away. He pointed and laughed: "Chinese n——as." I was curious where I fit into their typology, but not enough to ask.

I was one of the quieter mentors, and because I rarely told my mentees what to do—beyond never bringing a gun in my car ever again—I probably seemed nice, if a bit pliable. They cheerfully pushed me as far as they could. But I was a persistent presence and willing chauffeur. And once I started making fun of them for the way they dressed or wore their hair, we were good. Whenever a moment of earnestness accidentally opened up, I made them promises. So long as they worked hard and stayed in school, things would be fine. In the meantime, I'd keep taking them to the mall or to go see movies on weekends. Maybe they'd end up going to Berkeley, like all of us mentors.

Back on campus, the volunteers talked about what it meant to guide someone who was just a few years younger than us. Our primary authority derived from the fact that we were college students. But if college was just a way of reproducing privilege, one of my friends asked, why offer higher education as the answer to their problems? Why *should* we encourage them to go to college? Berkeley was 40 percent Asian at the time, but this mainly consisted of middle-class students whose families had come from Japan, South Korea, India, or the Chinese diaspora. For us, a public school like Berkeley represented a nice bargain, not a make-or-break lifeline. Our students in Richmond had been identified as at-risk youth. But they weren't just at risk of succumbing to specific ills, like gangs and drugs, which were ever present. The more general risk was that they would step into too much of the world too quickly—that they would never have the chance to discover their potential on their own terms, whatever that meant.

. .

In those early, barely governed days of the internet, the online world was manageably vast. It felt like a world you could master. There were only so many rooms to explore. You could spend a lot of time there, but not that much. Mostly, you realized that people were bored everywhere. We had come there to find others who were into the same, obscure things as us. People built websites, shrines to their heroes, who were obviously too cool to ever use computers. The internet was full of gifts, strangers offering each other candy, sharing with the like-minded and curious. Everything was sustained through generosity.

In the early twentieth century, the anthropologist Bronislaw Malinowski ventured to the Trobriand Islands, part of present-day Papua New Guinea, in order to study the region's practice of gift exchange. People of the islands would travel great distances to offer one another symbolic, seemingly worthless necklaces and armbands. Malinowski believed he was observing a kind of soft power. Gift exchange was not a form of altruism, since there was the expectation of reciprocity. And it wasn't random, since the flow of gifts followed discernible patterns. Instead, he argued that this act of giving and receiving bound everyone in a political process. The expansion of these exchanges across the islands represented an expansion of political authority.

The sociologist Marcel Mauss found Malinowski's explanation insufficient. He felt that Malinowski placed too much emphasis on transaction, rather than how feelings of indebtedness actually work. In 1923, he published "Essay on the Gift," which placed Malinowski's island networks in conversation with gifting practices in other societies, like indigenous traditions in the Americas, systems of communal ownership in China. Mauss introduced the idea of delayed reciprocity. You give expecting to receive. Yet we often give and receive according to intermittent, sometimes random intervals. That time lag is where a relationship emerges. Perhaps gifts serve political ends. But Mauss also believed that they strengthened the bonds between people and communities. Your obligation isn't just to repay the gift according to a one-to-one ratio. You're beholden to the "spirit of the gift," a kind of shared faith. Every gesture carries a desire for connection, expanding one's ring of associations.

It's not that we fancied ourselves somewhere free from the market, even though nobody I knew had any idea how you could make money off the internet. Was it in the ten bucks a month I paid for AOL? Everyone online shared their joy and esoteric knowledge. Someone made a web page about your favorite band; maybe you could go and make one about your second-favorite band. You posted a list of tapes for trade—not for sale. I used my zine as an excuse to quiz people in bands or influential listserv members about what they were doing with their lives, how they spent their free time, whether the majority of their friends were real or virtual. I never used any of the dollar bills people sent me for my zines. It was more than money.

Anthony was studying in Seville the fall of our junior year, so Ben, an affable white biology major from Ojai, moved in with little more than a drafting desk and a state-of-the-art, lightweight bicycle. Ben was always studying. Some nights, Ken and Sean came over, and we explored AOL's chat rooms together. Mostly, we logged in to the conservative ones. The people drawn to this chat felt isolated in some way, as though their environments had pushed them here, onto their computers, and then into the digital unknown, in search of connection. I created a different screen name, and we pretended to be an urbane, middle-aged white man, possibly a small-business owner. Everyone else in the room felt like a single alien out there, somewhere, ruing what society had become. We listened and agreed about how things were much better in our day. Then, as a solution, we proposed socialism. We laughed so hard at these old Americans that we cried.

I always felt as if my friends were sacrificing something by spending their precious Friday or Saturday nights this way. More often than not, I was at my computer anyway. But they could have all been out getting drunk, meeting girls, acting reckless. Instead, they were huddled around my computer, trash-talking strangers, and listening to my records. Between songs, when it was quiet, Ken's clock ticked away above us. Friends from down the hall would come home after a party or a date and see us there, wisecracking about "humane capitalism" in a chat room, and shake their heads in astonishment that this is how we'd chosen to spend our evening.

Eventually, we would fold ourselves into my car and drive to an all-night donut shop on San Pablo. I hated when my friends talked over my music, and I hated it even more when Ken led them in sing-alongs, replacing the perfect harmonies of "God Only Knows" with their wounded cadences. It was my car, but it was no longer my kingdom. Sean, Ben, and Ken delighted in singing loudly and out of tune.

At first, perhaps it was just to annoy me, three young men singing, one begging them to stop. But then it became a noise that felt safe, possibly better than the original. In the immediacy of the song, as its seconds tick away, you're experiencing it as a community—as a vision of the world vibrating together. It tickles your ear, then the rest of you, as your voice merges with everyone else's. The violent dissonance when someone, and then another, slips off-key, and everyone ventures off toward their own *ba-ba-baa* solo. I finally felt in my body how music worked. A chorus of nonbelievers, channeling God. A harmonic coming together capable of overtaking lyrics about drift and catastrophe, a song as proof that people can work together. We would sit in the parking lot until the song ended. The donuts weren't very good, but at least they provided a destination for our moving choir. We were sharing something, a combination of delirium and fraternity.

For months, Ken had patiently waited for a specific Abercrombie & Fitch jacket to come back into stock. It was blue with a broad cream stripe across the chest and a thinner red one inside that. The jacket was roomy, with a soft dark gray flannel lining. This specific color combination was sold out in the Bay Area, but he'd found an Abercrombie in San Diego, near the airport, that still had one in stock.

He explained all this to me as soon as he saw me at the baggage carousel. It was winter break of our junior year. I had just arrived in San Diego on an early morning flight from San Francisco. I really wanted to go back to sleep. It was dark when we took off, and it was only slightly less dark now. He assured me I could nap in the car. "We just have to stop by the mall." I registered my annoyance, and he began making fun of the thick, fur-lined military parka I was wearing. It was seventy-five degrees out. I'd bought the parka after finals, a couple days prior, and I convinced myself that it might be chilly enough to wear it on this trip, even though it was never not short sleeves weather down south.

We sat in the food court and waited for the rest of the mall to open. Ken had gone swing dancing the night before, and he was proud of his improving skills. He got home late, and his parents were asleep, but he somehow coaxed his mom out of bed to twirl with him. I listened, eating a cinnamon roll. Abercrombie finally opened, and I told him I would stay outside. I didn't want to break my streak of never having set foot in one. He walked out with a wide, satisfied grin. The jacket would match his new red Cuban Sugar Kings cap. It was only 10:00 a.m. and it was already a great day.

It was nice to be around someone else's parents—to be in a household with different defaults and codes. Having to finish all our food, no matter how much his mom kept piling on my plate. His dad cordially asking about my classes and major. At school, we felt grown up, now that we had declared our majors and mastered the basics of laundry and cooking. But crashing in Ken's childhood room reminded me of who we used to be. This small world where Ken was a mischievous son and annoying younger brother and I was his weird friend who'd worn a heavy winter jacket to San Diego. I wondered if I conformed to his descriptions of me. *Yes, ma'am, that's right. I'd like to be a researcher when I grow up.* It felt good to promise his mom that we were on our way somewhere.

Ken and I spent the next couple days driving around El Cajon, eating burritos from places that ended with "-berto's." Because he was driving, we listened to his music. Ken had taken up swing dancing after watching the movie *Swingers*. (I imagined this was the music they played inside Abercrombie.) He had just gotten the Cornershop CD, which I liked and which irritated his sister. When "Crash into Me" by Dave Matthews Band came on, I rolled my window up, in case anyone pulled up next to us at the light. It was dreadful. Still, I admired the way Ken got lost in his music, his life force mingling with Matthews's mumbles and sighs.

Ken took me to CD City, an oddly named, secondhand cassette shop in a strip mall. I found a Biz Markie tape but little else of note. He bought a Blues Brothers tape and the new Missy Elliott. As we drove in search of our next burrito, Busta Rhymes's "Dangerous" came on the radio. He asked if I'd seen the video, the one that parodied *The Last Dragon*. *Nah,* I said, *I don't really watch MTV anymore. And* The Last Dragon . . . *oh yeah, I've heard of that* (I had not). *I can't remember, though, it's been so long . . . Bruce Lee, right?* "You don't know who Sho'nuff is? Really? We'll watch it tonight," he assured me.

We stopped at a 7-Eleven late that night so Ken could buy cigarettes. It was still warm outside. I waited in the car and watched as he chatted with the clerk. It was like viewing a movie, the way the store glowed against the night sky. I leaned out the window to take a photo of the 7-Eleven sign. When he came back, Ken told me the clerk had asked him why the guy in the car was taking pictures. "It's probably for his zine," he responded, not bothering to explain.

The only place for me to roll out a sleeping bag was a thin gulch between the foot of Ken's enormous bed and his dresser, on top of which stood a large television. He assured me it was safe since, if the TV fell, there wasn't enough clearance for it to actually crush me. It was already well past midnight, and I had an early flight back to the Bay Area. But Ken dug out his VHS copy of *The Last Dragon*. The full title, for some reason, was actually *Berry Gordy's The Last Dragon*. I dug obscure, random things, and I wasn't all that interested in things that were popular, especially if I'd missed out on them the first time around. He promised me it would be worth it: "Let's just watch the beginning." I figured we would make it through the opening scene before nodding off.

After about ten minutes, I was convinced that *Berry Gordy's The Last Dragon* was the greatest movie ever made. It was a kung fu comedy that featured a predominantly Black cast, centered on a young man named Leroy Green—also known as Bruce LeeRoy—and his quest for "the Glow," a mystical energy that only the greatest martial artists are capable of wielding. Leroy is deeply confused about his own identity, wandering New York with a kind of ignorant bliss, as those around him gently question his blackness. He seems almost secretly Asian, because his spiritual journey takes him to the back alleys of Chinatown in search of the wise, secretive Master Sum Dum Goy, who he believes is the protector of "the Glow."

I was exhausted yet invigorated. I kept craning my neck to make sure Ken was still awake. *Are you seeing this?* I would ask. *Did you notice that?* He just nodded sagely, quietly satisfied that I now saw the light.

We had grown so accustomed to not seeing people who looked like us in the movies; worse was when a token Asian character was included as some kind of martial arts master. But as Leroy approaches the Master's quarters, some Chinese characters accuse him of being "jive," mocking his accent and kung fu fetish, their attitude and inflection borrowed from a blaxploitation flick. They were playing stereotypes, only the wrong ones. Then again, so was Leroy.

Who was copying whom? Did it matter? It turned out Master Sum Dum Goy was just a machine cranking out slips of faux wisdom for fortune cookies. The absurdity of it all was intoxicating, as was the sense that the film recognized something about being Asian American, even if that wasn't its core intention. During the slow moments, we kept trying to figure out where we located ourselves in the movie. On the one hand, we were rooting for Leroy, the Black hero obsessed with Asian culture. We were drawn to his conviction, as well as how out of place he felt. Yet it was just as thrilling to see these Chinese extras ham it up. The actors themselves seemed to break character, ecstatic at not having to play the overfamiliar role of a doctor or silent kung fu henchman. We eventually got to the part with Sho'nuff—the "Shogun of Harlem" referenced in the Busta Rhymes video.

The Last Dragon was a commentary on authenticity, the porousness of identity, the joyful, postmodern possibilities of mixing and matching Asian and Black cultures! Maybe it wasn't, but we stayed up well into morning dissecting it as though it held the key to our world. We kept saying good night, more of a joke than anything, and then raising one more point. *Were they making fun of Chinatown, or were they pointing out that there's nothing authentic about it?* I felt nauseated and overtired as I tried to spin a unified theory of American identity from this movie. Ken was quiet, possibly asleep, but just thinking. Then he would offer his own take. We came up with brilliant theories but forgot to write them down. I remember the orange-purple hue through his curtains—a shade of dawn I thought was natural until I moved east.

Friendship rests on the presumption of reciprocity, of drifting in and out of one another's lives, with occasional moments of wild intensity. When you're nineteen or twenty, your life is governed by debts and favors, promises to pick up the check or drive next time around. We built our lives into a set of mutual agreements, a string of small gifts lobbed back and forth. Life happened within that delay. I started a Secret Santa exchange, only I was anti-religion, and I didn't want to call it that, so it became known as the Secret Non-Denominational Winter Holiday Gift Giver. "We celebrate goodwill and brotherhood," I wrote, so no girls were invited. I scanned in all our pictures and made a flyer with the rules: no CDs and nothing that could be scammed from work, like "a spool of fax paper or children's shoes from Nordstrom." We were also supposed to pool together some money for charity. I imagined keeping this up into our forties.

I thought college was where I would find my people, which I assumed meant people who dressed like me, and listened to the same music as me, and wanted to see the same movies as me. Variations on the theme of me. But I realized, maybe too late, that all I wanted was friends to listen to music with. Someone curious enough to ask what something was and then recipro- cate by playing me something by Styx or Christopher Cross or another artist I was far too cool to know. Ken devoured the tapes I made him and then, like an encouraging parent, offered a song-by-song critique. I joked that he was probably the only frat boy in America to like Belle and Sebastian's meekest tunes. He left my tapes strewn about, on the floor of his car or in some dusty corner of the frat house, knowing there would be a new edition soon, requesting repeats of favorites—"the song about the horses."

Everybody likes something—a song, a movie, a TV show—so you choose not to; this is how you carve out space for yourself. But the right person persuades you to try it, and you feel as though you've made two discoveries. One is that this thing isn't so bad. The other is a new confidant.

Ken told me how he had driven all over San Diego in search of the CD single for Pearl Jam's "Jeremy" because of a song called "Yellow Ledbetter." I rolled my eyes as aggressively as possible. Clearly a rip-off of a Jimi Hendrix song. I dug through my records trying to find "Little Wing," but Ken was elsewhere, following the song's fluttering guitar line, remembering a girl for whom he'd played it. Eventually, we struck a compromise. Before our finals, we would sit in front of my stereo and rever- ently listen to "Yellow Ledbetter." It wasn't so bad. Then my choice, David Bowie and Queen's "Under Pressure," would rouse us out the door. We lived for rituals, looking forward to the day when they would be so instinctive that we would forget how they started. There was still time to repay these gifts.

THE RAPA - NUI
2150

A SPORE TAKES FLIGHT BY WIND, and the whole system survives. The assassin blinks, and the bullet merely grazes the head of state. The planet's axis shifts imperceptibly, and Earth is ruled by some other species. It's not even called Earth; there is no language at all. The letter is lost in the mail, the opportunity gone forever.

All my classes in college essentially taught the same lesson: another world was once possible. This realization is meant to be humbling. The scholar consults the past, rooting around in an archive, or the imperiled practices of some remote tribe, all in the hope of adding a page to the book of human knowledge. Those histories uplift and sustain us. But they also cast the present in fatalistic light, a sense that things could have been different, now, if only we had once known the small dangers lining the paths we walked.

Although Marcel Mauss first published "Essay on the Gift," his classic work on the "spirit" that bound the gift giver to the recipient, in the 1920s, it wasn't widely available in translation to American scholars until the early 1950s. It became a canonical work, reprinted as a slim, stand-alone book. Generations of thinkers would consult Mauss's insights into practices of exchange that might have evolved into capitalism, but somehow did not.

When "Essay on the Gift" was originally published in 1923, it was part of a special issue of *L'Année sociologique,* a journal that Émile Durkheim, Mauss's mentor, had founded in 1896, overseeing it until his death, in 1917. Because of Durkheim's passing and World War I, the journal had been dormant until Mauss took it over in 1923. The return issue overseen by Mauss is nearly one thousand pages long, and his essay is the only original work of scholarship. It is surrounded by nearly nine hundred pages of other materials that seem unrelated yet hint at the ethos that might have animated Mauss's thinking.

This issue of *L'Année sociologique* paid tribute to a generation of scholars who were among the millions lost over the preceding decade. It begins with a lengthy "In Memoriam" section. "We will never lose from view that there existed among us a true sharing of the work. The example of our dead will be a model."

There is Robert Hertz, a scholar of religion, who "was killed in the useless attack of Marchéville, April 13, 1915, at the age of thirty-three, leading his section out of the trench." Maxime David died in combat, in 1914, leaving behind copious and no doubt "excellent" notes about ancient Greek literature. Jean Reynier "ran the same dangers as his friends" but died at the age of thirty-two from an accident involving a trench engine. He is remembered for the "remarkable" lectures he gave on asceticism. Antoine Bianconi "had sketched out a great work" but died in 1915 leading his section of the infantry. Georges Gelly, a philosopher and philologist, defied death many times until "one day in 1918 took him away from us."

Mauss projects into a future that never arrived, imagining "what this would have become, if there had been no war" and his colleagues had continued living and working together. "Let us imagine that Gelly had become our expert in aesthetics, and that André Durkheim had become our linguist." Their names are unknown to the generations of students who followed. Mauss compels us to know them as thinkers as well as friends—to hold on to the possibilities of what could have been.

In this context, Mauss's idea of the gift takes on a new resonance. He's not just speculating about alternatives to market-driven systems of exchange; he dreams of an entirely different way of living. He is salvaging a lost world, trying to see through on a set of impossible potentialities. When Mauss turns his discussion of gifts to gestures of "generosity" or speaks of sitting together "around the common wealth," he is trying to remind us that there are other ways of being than that of "economic man." That remnants of "another law, another economy, and another mentality" survive alongside the ones we perceive to be inevitable and final.

It's remarkable to think that this is where his personal ghosts have delivered him, to this moment of hope. To follow through on the work, Mauss suggests, is the debt we owe these fallen colleagues. His essay chases a string of gifts around the world and through the deep, historical past in order to remind you about the possibilities of where you stand. "It is useless to go looking for goodness and happiness far away," he concludes. They're closer than you think.

Mauss and the other survivors of this tumultuous stretch of human history are like the "devastated" part of the woods where, for a few years, some old trees "try to become green again." Something more capricious than a gift changing hands. Something more mysterious than an ornamental necklace or carving. Something more like seeds, carried by the wind, falling and germinating.

Whatever may come: "let us work a few more years."

One night, Ken grabbed a legal pad and drove us to a café. After watching *The Last Dragon,* we were inspired to try to make our own movie. His working title was *Barry Gordy's IMBROGLIO.* "Barry Gordy" was an homage to *The Last Dragon.* "Imbroglio" was just a funny word. I knew who Berry Gordy was and how to properly spell his name, but I chose not to lord this knowledge over Ken.

He wrote out the main characters and listed sitcoms from our childhood, some familiar TV themes and tropes; we had to figure out our own twist on these narrative conventions. It revolved around a bunch of friends, a collection of self-conscious archetypes: the nice but misunderstood protagonist; the hot, soulful sidekick and the vain, arrogant one; the level-headed sophisticate with the steady girlfriend and sage advice; the wisecracking cynic, who thought all of his friends were philistines.

We cast our friends: Anthony, Paraag, and Dave. Sammi, Alec, and Gwen. Ken wrote a part for James, one of my high school friends, who was going to art school in San Diego. We'd hung out with him during my visit to El Cajon. We invented roles for girls we liked—nothing more than passive-aggressive lust, maybe some handholding. He jotted down some scenes and settings drawn from our own experiences. That time I smoked the wrong end of a cigarette and then claimed that I'd done it on purpose. That one sandwich place with the awkward, deeply impractical, triangular tables. We would make *Barry Gordy's IMBROGLIO* and find an empty lecture hall on campus to screen it for our friends. We didn't want to be filmmakers; we just wanted to make something, to discover if such a thing was possible. We just needed to find someone with a camcorder.

My parents were spending more time in Taiwan. I had prepaid phone card numbers written everywhere, but I could never remember which ones worked, or which country and city codes to dial. Sean, like me, was an only child, and he spoke to his parents every single day. My parents would tell me their schedules, but I never kept close enough track of their whereabouts. I would go weeks having no idea whether they were in Hsinchu or weekending in Taipei.

My father often referred to himself as "Eastern" or "Oriental." He didn't get why it was so important to call ourselves "Asian American," a term that barely existed when he first arrived in the United States. My parents recognized the names of some of the older Chinese American professors in the Ethnic Studies Department. I asked if they had any memories of the Black Panthers or if they'd been aware of the Yellow Power movement of the late 1960s. Their answers were always vague. That was a long time ago, they'd say, and we were busy.

I told them about all the protests and rallies at Berkeley, the late-night hours I was spending on the Asian American newspaper on campus. I thought they'd be proud. But they didn't understand why these were distinctions worth fighting for. I was sympathetic, reflecting on their struggles back when they arrived—my mother's isolation, my dad getting mugged on his first day in New York. I was grateful they had made these sacrifices for me. "For you?" my dad said with a laugh. "We came for ourselves. There was nothing in Taiwan when we left."

My parents would drive great distances to have meals with their friends, whom they always referred to as part of "the movement." Whenever I asked what this meant, they chuckled and used a Chinese phrase that roughly translates to "the left side." The part that they stressed was how the movement had diverted their focus; the movement was why it took my father longer than it should have to finish graduate school, much to the chagrin of his patient doctoral advisers. They feared that these extracurricular activities were distracting me from my schoolwork, too.

When my parents left Taiwan back in their twenties, the country was still under martial law—the result of violence in the late 1940s as Chinese nationalists assumed control of the island, silencing dissent among the native Taiwanese people. Politics hadn't been a part of my parents' lives growing up. But watching the cold war play out from afar emboldened them to think and say things that might have gotten them in trouble had they stayed home. They became involved in activism, much of it focused on a small, uninhabited, possibly resource-rich string of islands claimed by both Taiwan and Japan. In the early 1970s, my parents traveled to colleges throughout the Midwest and East Coast, and my father would smoke cigarettes and angrily debate other students about the Tiao Yu Tai Islands. He was critical of Taiwan's official position, which conceded too much to Japan. Word got back to Taiwan, and the story was that he was not allowed to return for about twenty years.

The era of martial law, dubbed the White Terror, lasted until the late 1980s as Taiwan began to reassess its history. My father was finally able to go back as part of a wave of Taiwanese who were bringing their business and engineering expertise back home to the island's nascent semiconductor industry. He was hailed as a kind of returning hero. When they told me they'd once been just like me, all the protests and planning meetings, debates and rallies, I refused to believe them. I couldn't even picture him smoking. They were trying to shield me from something. Maybe it was the possibility of disappointment that attends idealism. Nobody cared about the Tiao Yu Tai Islands anymore, and that work had taken so much time and energy. What they had to show for their work, I thought, was their friends.

I wasn't a particularly great mentor to the kids in Richmond. I had very little to offer them; I simply wanted to be liked. Yet when the center announced that they were looking to hire a summer school teacher, I jumped at the opportunity. I still imagined that teaching would be a meaningful backup plan if I graduated from college without any clearly marketable skills. Teaching required an earnestness I didn't yet feel comfortable projecting, and I wanted to get better at it.

I was more comfortable composing my thoughts in private, dragging a blinking cursor across a screen. I still wrote little missives for my zine, and I started a second zine that was about crushes and unrequited fixations. I had found a community. Nights were spent editing the campus paper or going to strategy sessions, where we painted protest signs, debated the future of California, taught one another that it was always harder for the police to drag away a limp body. Assembling zines had taught me some basics of graphic design, so I always volunteered to make flyers or lay out manifestos. It was a way of delaying questions about a practical, boring future. Maybe my zine, and these assorted design jobs, would attest to my entrepreneurialism, if proof of such a trait ever became necessary.

Near the end of junior year, Ken and I were smoking on his balcony when I told him about Mira, a Taiwanese American girl from Southern California who worked on the campus paper with me. A few weeks earlier, she had asked to catch a ride with me to Davis, where I was on a panel about Asian American DIY culture. I found her intimidatingly hot. I spent days making a mixtape versatile enough to communicate my humor, depth, and compassion. After that weekend, Mira and I kept hanging out, mostly listening to music and watching movies. I was obsessed with the auburn tint of her hair, the abundance of loops when she wrote in cursive, the way she spelled really "rilly." Sometimes, we drove to a diner in San Francisco and, because she was a vegetarian, ate a dinner of fries and ice cream. We would lie on the ground underneath Coit Tower and stare up at the stars, never quite touching. Near the end of the semester, I skipped classes and drove to Los Angeles for a conference where the activists Yuri Kochiyama and Grace Lee Boggs were speaking together. Mira flew down, too, and I offered to pick her up. But we couldn't find each other at the airport. We kept missing each other's pages. I worried that there was some symbolism to our failed connection.

When we finally saw each other that night at the conference, I told her that I cared for her. We sat in a lecture hall, inspired by the thinkers and political leaders around us, awed that Grace and Yuri were just a few feet away. I looked at Mira and felt as if we were part of something. We could build a new world together.

Mira mistook my shyness and general cluelessness as cool nonchalance. Back in Berkeley, we finally confessed to liking each other. It took another all-night hang until I felt uninhibited enough to try to kiss her. We were gentle and deliberate with each other, and then, as the sun rose, we fell asleep from exhaustion. Now we were together, whatever that meant.

I felt a little anxious recounting all this to Ken, since I tended to disappear into my infatuations with girls. I'd been ducking him during my slow-motion courtship of Mira. He always seemed to understand whenever something like this happened. Whenever I had a girlfriend, I was even harder than usual to reach. But this time felt different. For our first date, I'd taken Mira to see an independent film that involved a bunch of restless punks suffering through awful one-night stands. A few days later, we saw *Kids*. All of it made sex seem bleak and terrifying, and because I was still a virgin, I wasn't in any great hurry to find out otherwise. We had so much time, and I loved every second of getting to know her, exploring her tape collection, talking about our memories of visiting Taiwan, recalling the many times our paths probably crossed back when she worked the floor at Rasputin Music on Telegraph. Every day suddenly felt novel and exciting.

Ken was happy that Mira and I were hanging out. In fact, he knew her and had been meaning to set us up; her roommate was Charles, one of his frat brothers. Ken beamed like a proud, approving father that I'd gone and done it myself.

I had never felt so young, and Ken had never seemed so old. The Multicultural Student Alliance had run its course, and he'd given up on abstruse theory. He'd come up with something called the International Regulatory Trade Commission for a class paper, and he thought it was a pretty good idea. He sketched out a vision of law school in Boston, nights spent selling concessions at Fenway Park. Ken seemed slightly vexed about his future, or maybe he was just ready for it, and it required a requisite level of seriousness. He was dating a Chinese American sorority girl who projected a similarly down-to-earth focus. She would pack him snacks for our library study sessions. We still did our silly handshake, the one we'd come up with as freshmen on the Unit 3 balcony. But he was suddenly like a proper adult, more interested in sophistication than coolness, conjuring visions of a productive, postcollege life.

Most of us stayed in Berkeley that summer. Ken still had his job selling children's shoes at Nordstrom. He got his manager to hire Sammi, too, and they'd take the BART to San Francisco together. Anthony was working part time for the university and at a nonprofit. Paraag had somehow persuaded a sports agency in San Francisco to bring him on as an intern, even though it didn't offer internships. Mira was taking summer classes.

I was going to Richmond every morning to teach the youth center's fifth and sixth graders writing, math, and history. They were the younger brothers and sisters of the mentees I already knew, though that one- or two-year gap meant that they were still sweet and innocent. Their older siblings had come to like me, but maybe these kids would actually listen to me. I dutifully copied worksheets and exercises, carefully mapped out every block of our mornings together. But I could never summon any of the gravitas necessary to give our days shape or flow. I lesson-planned questions that unfolded into other questions, and then I'd lose my nerve at the first sign of someone looking out the window. Soon, they realized I wasn't just a poor teacher; I was also a pushover—a rude awakening to the reality that sometimes adults didn't know what was going on either. I could pretend to be an authority for only so long. They danced and listened to music. The boundaries between the boys and the girls began blurring as they would furtively tickle or wrestle one another.

In late June, I turned twenty-one. Mira met me in Richmond; her presence made me appear more respectable in my students' eyes, and one of them drew a picture of her festooned with hearts. She took me out to lunch at a nearby diner, and she presented me with a zine about our relationship. There were ticket stubs to movies and concerts, business cards from restaurants we'd gone to, diary entries from the early days, poems about our future, memories of how she saw through all my attempts to flirt in nonobvious ways.

That evening, my friends met us in San Francisco for my birthday dinner. Anthony, Alec, and Gwen came from Berkeley. Paraag was already in the city. I sat at the head of the table and felt a little sentimental about how long it had been since we'd all hung out together. Maybe we were drifting apart, toward the different paths slowly coming into focus. Or maybe this was just a lull in the natural rhythm of friendship. In either case, we were now old enough to order appetizers. Ken and Sammi were late. They came straight from the department store. Ken's blazer, and the way he worked the table, laughing and shaking hands, made him seem like an affable game show host. He gave Mira a gentlemanly hug and ended with me, grinning before giving me a forceful backslap. He took a seat and scanned the menu, quickly deciding on the most unusual item available: roasted rabbit.

Ken tried to rally us to go swing dancing after dinner, but I told him I'd never do such a thing, let alone on my birthday. He was always asking, and I was always putting him off. *Some other time . . . maybe.* He disappeared to the bar, and I wondered if my snootiness toward his new hobby had finally pissed him off. But he returned with a smile and a shot glass for me. He chuckled as I began slowly sipping it; I'd never been handed a shot before, and I'd only recently started to feel okay about drinking. "It's a Three Wise Men," he explained, slapping me on the back again. "Jack, Johnnie, Jim Beam. Just down it!"

.   .   .

The seasons of keggers and ragers were now over. Three weeks later, Ken threw a housewarming party. Calling it that, as opposed to simply a party, signaled our arrival at adulthood. He was moving into the Rapa-Nui, an apartment building up the street where Gwen already lived. The following month, we would be seniors.

Anthony, Mira, and I were going to a rave in Oakland later that night. We showed up at Ken's party early, which seemed reasonable given the event's civilized nature, but it's possible we were still too early; one of his new roommates had his homework open in his lap. I was glad to be able to hang out with Ken before the party picked up, but I felt guilty knowing we would bail early. He greeted us warmly. *I need a smoke,* I whispered. We disappeared to christen his new balcony, which overlooked the building's parking lot.

I needed Ken's counsel. After an awkward, aborted attempt at sex, I was finally ready to lose my virginity, and I raised this to him, half expecting him to joke about how comically long it had taken me to get here. I was, indeed, alternative to the core. He smiled and gently punched my shoulder. I laughed, thinking about all the times I nodded along to his stories of dates or hookups, as though I had the faintest sense of what he was talking about.

We smoked with our normal sense of ritualistic purpose. We were serious about being serious. I imagined smoking many cigarettes on this balcony in the year to come. Ken was about to tell me something when the sliding doors opened and Daniel, a lanky science major whom Sammi had recently started dating, came out onto the balcony. We talked about Daniel's summer job in a campus lab. Ken leaned over and put his arm around him, bringing him close. Sammi's the best, he said, and she deserves to be treated that way. Daniel looked at Ken, nodded, and went back inside. Then someone else came out and told us about a device called a CD burner. Ken was intrigued, but I rolled my eyes. Who cared about CDs when it was easier to make tapes?

We were in the middle of something, and then we weren't. I was annoyed, but I had other plans anyway. I left my cigarette to die a natural death on the edge of the railing, wondering if it would eventually smolder and ash onto the cars below us. I still needed advice, but I told Ken we'd resume this smoke later.

"I'll call you Sunday," he said. "This guy at work. It's his birthday. He doesn't have many friends, and I thought it would be cool if we took him out dancing." He meant swing dancing, so I was immediately uninterested. *I don't even know the guy,* I said. *Who is the "we" here?* He grimaced. "It would be a nice thing to do, man." *Yeah, sure . . . call me tomorrow,* I said, hoping he'd forget.

I had to leave, but maybe I'd drive by later and see if the party was still going.

At first, I was drawn to raves more for the idea of community than the music itself. You found a flyer, called a number, copied down the directions. It meant surrendering to a void, a cluster of headlights the signal you were in the right place. I never did drugs, but it still felt magical to be in a room with no center, where the only way of orienting yourself was by following a bass line or synth wash. This was a range of faces you didn't see in daytime: vacant and somber, devoted to the rhythm; smiling and platonic, eager to share; rapturously free. Something was always already happening. People walked in casually, and their gait slowly adapted to the sounds around them, and within minutes they looked as though they were trying to punch and kick their way out of an imaginary sack. It didn't matter how you danced.

That night, Anthony, Mira, and I went to Planet Rock, a party that took place at the International Trade Center, a large warehouse next to the Oakland Coliseum. We agreed to check in at a designated meeting place at around three, though I don't think we were ever separated by more than a few feet. Nothing sounded good that night. The space was at once wide open and suffocating. As night became early morning, I remember an unshakable humidity, standing in a hangar where you could hear too many of the sound systems at once, the psychedelic aura smothered by gray clouds, a drifting weariness. For a flash, I no longer felt young.

We stayed until three or four. After dropping Anthony off,

Mira and I drove back to her place, passing Ken's balcony. The lights were still on. I remembered the conversation we had paused and contemplated stopping by. But I thought he'd appreciate my haste to get to Mira's. I'd tell him about this milestone later.

On Monday afternoon, Sammi asked if I'd talked to Ken. *Yeah.* "Have you talked to him since his party?" *No.* He hadn't called on Sunday to go dancing with his co-worker. Sammi said that he hadn't shown up at work that day, either. Maybe he'd gotten into a fight with his girlfriend? No, Sammi continued, she hasn't heard from him either. Nobody knew where he was.

I walked over to the apartment Sammi shared with Alec, passing the Rapa-Nui on the way. Derrick, one of Ken's frat brothers, was already there. They had called the police to file a missing person's report. Alec had just poured a bowl of Raisin Bran when I arrived.

An officer from the Berkeley Police Department pulled up. I looked at his badge and memorized his name. He was calm and deliberate as he asked us questions. It was as if he were performing some awful magic trick, randomly conjuring bits of Ken-related trivia but never naming him. Did we know anyone who might have been wearing a faded Ned's Used Books T-shirt and brown boots that weekend? Did we have any friends who owned a necklace made of white shells? Anyone you know drive a 1991 Honda Civic? The questions grew teasingly intimate, and then he stopped. Would a couple of you come with me to the station? he asked.

Sammi and Derrick went with the police officer, while Alec and I sat on the steps, smoking. We didn't know what to feel quite yet. Alec's cereal was soggy by now, our only indication of time passing. It was too much to contemplate the worst; we were on the verge of any number of possible futures. A cheerful Samoan dude from my ethnic studies classes walked by, and I wondered where he was going, how anyone could be going anywhere right now.

We were still sitting on the porch a couple hours later, when a police car dropped Sammi and Derrick off. She was pale. Derrick shuffled behind her, his eyes fixed to the ground. Sammi told us that Ken was dead. Derrick put his arm around me. I could feel him standing there, stiff and upright, trying to stay strong, and I buried my face in his shoulder, sobbing. "He's gone, Hua," he whispered.

Ken's body had been found in an alleyway in Vallejo, about thirty minutes north. Between here and there, a zigzag of attempted ATM withdrawals. A fisherman had come across Ken's body early Sunday morning. Ken had no identification, and his car was still missing, so he was initially a John Doe. An artist's rendering of his face had been posted around campus the day before.

I thought about how I'd left his party early, passing his balcony, how relieved I felt on Sunday night that he hadn't called to go dancing.

It was still sunny. I left them and went to Mira's and told her the barest outline of what had happened. I drew the curtains; we had sex in almost total silence. Afterward, I went into the hallway and began calling my friends. It offered some weird sense of purpose to be the bearer of bad news and then the receptacle for another's pain. I was a storyteller with a plot twist guaranteed to astound and destroy.

I ended up back at my apartment, and I called his mom. Her voice was quivery and rough. There would be a funeral on Saturday in El Cajon. We should all come. "Kenny loved you," she said, and I collapsed to the ground, crying and pounding my fists in the carpet. "He admired you so much." Everyone came over that night. Our bodies shook from exhaustion, and we gorged ourselves on pizza and beer. Anthony kept staring off into the distance, his mouth agape. Alec was still in disbelief. Our lives had always seemed like a quirky yet uneventful indie movie to Gwen, and now, she said, it was over.

Over the next couple days, we dug out old photo negatives for a collage, jotted down any memories appropriate for sharing with his family. I went for a walk, distressed each time I saw someone smiling or laughing. I ended up at a clothing store, where I bought a pair of pin-striped pants—the kind I imagined people wore when they went swing dancing—and a black bowling shirt, for the same reason. It was not conventional funeral attire, but it seemed fitting. I also bought a journal. It had a dark blue fabric cover, with a dragon embroidered in gold. I began writing down everything I could remember. *Everything is wrong,* I scrawled in Sharpie across the first page.

Henry, one of our friends from the dorms, recorded a nightly news segment about Ken's death and made dubs for everyone. I crafted his parents an annotated mixtape of the songs that reminded me of their son. Anthony arranged our flights to San Diego for the funeral, distracting himself in the logistics of ensuring that all our friends, most of whom were in Berkeley and Los Angeles for the summer, ended up at the same place. He printed out and distributed an itinerary with a schedule of the weekend, addresses, whose car had how many seats, emergency contact numbers.

The police mentioned a credit card charge at a nearby mall. Henry jumped in his car and drove over to see if there was any surveillance footage. It felt as if the authorities weren't moving fast enough. Maybe Henry would crack the case first. But the killers weren't masterminds, and they didn't appear to have any plans for escape. They had made a scene when leaving the mall, and the police had little trouble piecing together what had happened. When they arrived to make the arrest, Ken's car was parked on their front lawn, its lights still on.

There had been three of them. A young couple and a man they had met at the Berkeley BART station. They had waited across the street from the party, watching people come and go, waiting for their moment, watching that lit balcony, waiting for a lone straggler. Ken was coming down the back stairwell to the parking lot in the early hours of Sunday morning when they came upon him. He did what they asked. He got into the trunk. He gave them his bank cards. Nevertheless, they drove him to Vallejo and shot him through the back of the head.

The day after Ken died, I stopped listening to songs from a specific zone of memory, avoided vibrations that reminded me of a certain register of feeling. Harmony was forbidden; it no longer made sense to me. I started spending less time with anyone who could evoke the past. I started wearing Nikes again, and Polo shirts, and backward baseball caps. Mostly, I became obsessed with the possibility of a sentence that could wend its way backward.

I picked up a pen and tried to write myself back into the past.

a call for submission

Slant

An Asian Pacific American magazi
all interested undergraduates/grad
dents to submit any original pie

politics	society and
film	music
opinion	arts and th
fiction/poetry	news
artwork	photograp

Works must be on issues and events
Asian Pacific American community. F
free to contact us and pitch story id
assignments, or get information on
with the *Slant* staff.

Submissions sh
cover page with your name, year i
title of work, telephone number, addres
copies of your work. Please drop off s
the *Slant* box at Heller Lounge on the
ASUC.

For more information or to cor
e-mail jojoba@uclink2 or huascene@a
a note in our box in Heller at the ASU

**deadline:
nov. 5 1997**

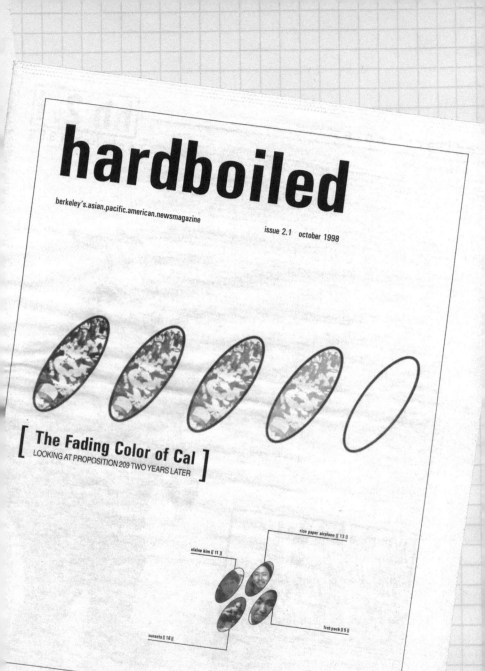

hardboiled

berkeley's.asian.pacific.american.newsmagazine

issue 2.1   october 1998

[The Fading Color of Cal]
LOOKING AT PROPOSITION 209 TWO YEARS LATER

THERE WAS A TIME when fragments would come spilling out of me a few sips into the first beer. The fact that this specific bottle I had chosen—Newcastle Brown Ale—reminded me of him. The fact that I was drinking at all. The fact that I had a tendency to disappear, to take friendship too seriously sometimes or not seriously at all most of the time. That my mood depended on the proximity to summertime, the feeling of the afternoon sun, the sound of a distant melody coming from a stranger's window. That this is why I still smoked, because I admired the way that smoke evaporated into the air, aimless and ephemeral.

The fact that in those early years, when our faces hadn't yet changed, I could picture Ken turning twenty-one, sitting in a lecture hall, graduating from college with a sensible haircut. Living in Boston, enrolled in law school, selling concessions at Fenway Park, as one of his many dreams used to go. The fact that I was a writer at all. A way to loot and hoard in a city on fire, to impose structure on chaos, to download the contents of a storage drive before it succumbed to corruption. Songs, notable T-shirts, and quotations from friends, written in the margins of my books. Taking a bar napkin to scribble down words, the dutiful, surviving half of an inside joke. I would tell you all this because it was my way of coping, of telling stories, of thinking that stories could build a bridge over an abyss.

Maybe it was legacy, a way of bringing Ken into this moment, a spirit made real in the clink of two bottles, the magical appearance of a sad song in the air.

· ·

College is filled with comings and goings, new apartments, each an opportunity to reboot your personality and surroundings. Life is too fast for too much preciousness, and soon after finals you pack up some stuff to send home, or you simply toss it out. Ken told me that he had once flung his Texas Longhorns cap through the sunroof of a passing limo. It was the year his beloved San Diego Chargers made it all the way to the Super Bowl—reason enough for a parade. This struck me as sad, since my Niners had trounced them in the big game. It wasn't even close. But Ken was there anyway, cheering on his heroes, and somehow the cap flew back to him with a dotted loop across the brim. He assured me it was Stan Humphries's autograph. When I came across it in my apartment a few days after, I found it upsetting you could spend so much time with someone and not realize how small their head was.

That first night, after everyone had gone home, I typed a letter to him detailing everything I would miss—his *soft skin and flatulence,* our routines and inside jokes. I listed things he'd left behind, because he was always leaving things behind: the bandage affixed to the air freshener in my car, the lucky volleyball shirt still in my hamper in Cupertino. All that I'd learned about loyalty, time-travel, treating a hangover with steak, eggs, and a side of pancakes. The screen names of the right-wing adults we used to ridicule on AOL ("TruthGator"). I told him about that night with Mira, how Gwen and Alec were holding up, how much we needed him back. *So be with me, okay, Ken? Can you stay with me a little longer?*

I didn't volunteer to deliver the eulogy, but the fact that I was constantly writing that week, engaged in a kind of showy archivalism, made me seem like the natural choice. It displaced some of my grief to feel the stress of an impending deadline.

In those first few days, everything assumed a talismanic significance. It was comforting to be around his things: T-shirts and hats, cassettes, a few pages from *Barry Gordy's IMBROGLIO*. His roommates invited us over, and I went to the balcony and grabbed the last pack of cigarettes we had been smoking.

It felt so good to wake up each morning. I opened my eyes, shook off my covers, and walked into our living room. For a fugitive moment, I forgot. I wondered why there were pizza boxes and wads of tissue all over my desk, why we hadn't bagged up all the beer bottles. I loved that feeling—that in-between state of not knowing, not remembering, just for a second.

We ate out a lot that week. Nobody was ever alone; every dinner was a party. We would share memories, verging downward, and then someone would recall something funny, pulling us back from the precipice. Paraag, Jen, Rosa, and I were eating noodles at King Dong, a Chinese restaurant. I remember leaning back in my chair and laughing as thunderously as physically possible. We were boisterous and loud, because we needed to be. I revealed Ken's secrets, telling our friends the things he adored about them. I told girls he secretly loved that he had loved them. I felt like an executor of his spiritual estate, parsing out wisdom or delight. And I wanted to be told the same kinds of stories.

I kept thinking about how eager I'd been to leave that night. I could still remember what the lights looked like as we drove by on our way to Mira's. I believed I had somehow allowed all this to happen.

I wrote him things that were crass and profane, silly and accusatory, broken and desperate, just to see if he could read from a great distance. I told him about sex and confusion and how his mother broke my heart in her attempts to comfort me. At the end of each night, I wrote it all down, because I never wanted to forget any of it—the ache, the release, the flashes of euphoria when we were all laughing together. On some pages, I disguised my handwriting, seeing if my squiggles would lead somewhere continuous and unbroken. My handwriting changed that week, growing curvier and more ornate, like the violent fury of graffiti tags. I got lost while searching for the right words. What was that thing we had learned in our rhetoric class, about Derrida's "deferral of meaning" and how words are merely signs that can never fully summon what they mean? Yet words are all we have, simultaneously bringing us closer, casting us farther away.

We decided the eulogy would be a collective effort. Anyone could share a memory or a feeling, and I would put it all together. "Ken had just met some of our high school friends," Rosa and Jen wrote on a napkin, "but that didn't stop him from sticking up for them when a bunch of guys picked a fight with them. Ken fought the hardest." There was a scrap of notepaper about how he was a "big little kid," unconscious poetry about never-to-be-used CD-Rs jotted on the back of a receipt.

There were two flights from Oakland to San Diego, and I was on the second one, which arrived at around 8:30 the night before the funeral. Moving as a pack felt essential. Everything seemed like a movie that week, the outline of friends against the orange-purple brilliance of dusk. We packed into a van waiting to take us to a motel.

I sat up front and started chatting with the van's driver; it felt strangely soothing to talk to a new person after a few days where the sight of another's unhappiness could send you spiraling. He was a big, curious man; it was apparent he actually relished the part of his job that involved socializing. There was a self-help book on his dashboard. But we were unusually quiet given the size of our party. After I explained the reason for our trip, he left us to ourselves, occasionally glancing at different faces through the rearview mirror.

We packed into a bank of rooms on the second floor of the motel. There were about a dozen of us. The first thing we did was move the chairs onto the balcony, so there'd be somewhere to smoke, and push together all the beds. We wondered what it would be like to attend a funeral for someone our age. Who else was coming? Did anyone know his parents? What's his sister like? I stayed up late trying to write. We slept soundly atop each other, blissful and clean.

That was the week flies were everywhere. Maybe it was the same one, following me wherever I went. Lying in bed or driving in a car with the windows up. In the cabin of an airplane, on the tip of a cigarette, on whatever balcony I found myself on. *I remember the way we all rubbed off on the guy,* I wrote in my blue journal, *I got a nic habit in return.* A fly landed on the page and walked across, its trail a sentence I could not read.

I obsessed over chronicling everything, noting all the atmospheric weirdness. In the margins of my journal, I drew a picture of the motel's trellis. I wrote as much as I could remember. Some of it was for future study, cryptic placeholder sentences about bygone times that felt too good for my present vocabulary. I wrote out of a sense of responsibility for our past. Some pages were filled with inside jokes, because I didn't want to forget what the "Great Egg Fiasco" was, or which of Ken's friends could never remember that my name wasn't "Woo."

On Saturday afternoon, we were allowed to view Ken's body. I wasn't done with the eulogy yet. I felt a sense of déjà vu as we drove down the street to the funeral home. Maybe it was the weather. I was with Anthony and the guys. We milled around in the parking lot for as long as we could, delaying the inevitable, our arms around one another, huddled as if we were getting ready for a big play. It felt safe, and we took turns reassuring one another that we would stay friends forever. Days had been spent summoning his essence, recalling his gaze and mannerisms and smells, and now his body was just a few yards away. We took turns approaching Ken's parents, who comforted us one by one. Their faces were swollen and creased. Then each of us approached the casket to pay respects, looking at our friend one last time, sharing one last intimacy. As I walked toward him, I couldn't shake off a curiosity: Would we be able to see the wound in his head, where the bullet must have exited? *Fuckin' Ken,* I whispered as I peered in. A fly landed on his cheek. I waved my hand, nearly touching him, yet it stayed put, as though taunting me.

Were all these omens and signs real? I became convinced all these flies were somehow him, buzzing around and messing with me, and I let out a hysterical laugh.

After changing back at the motel, we drove to a Wendy's around the corner. I curled up in a booth with my blue journal, trying to finish the eulogy, when a fly landed and walked across the lines I'd just written. It stopped. I drew a circle around it and smiled.

The service was at seven, though the day felt like one long, perfectly still afternoon. On the cover of the program was a small color picture of him. He looks as if he were about to see right through you. Underneath, the words "Love Lost, but Not Forgotten." It was standing room only. There were ecstatic tremors as I scanned the room. I saw Mira, whom I hadn't talked to in a few days and who hadn't told me she was coming. I felt a sudden, mad rush of love for her. An elder from Ken's church said he had never seen so many people at a funeral service. I was reminded that Ken had all these other identities: "Kenny," a member of the Greater San Diego Japanese American community, a little brother. A San Francisco newspaper had described him as "a scholar, Sigma Alpha Mu fraternity member and volleyball player who recently took up swing dancing." They referred to him as "Kenneth" and quoted friends I didn't know. I knew him in such a specific way ("Hiroshi Yamasaki"), and it began to feel too small. There were floral offerings from his high school friends, brothers in the fraternity, well-wishers from their family church. His family had set up a scholarship fund. I hadn't even known that he had a family church.

It wasn't just about us. We were simply his friends. We had known only slivers of him, for a few years of our relatively short lives.

The funeral felt like being at a rave. It was stuffy; I could see the air in the room moving. Everyone touching and swaying, leaning on your neighbor, emitting auras, alone in our own private worlds, desperate to enter into another one, together. A pained smile across the room could destroy you. The joyous throb and tingle of laughing together. Bodies trying to expel something wicked through fidgeting, sobbing, rocking back and forth in the pews, trying to rein it back in. I wanted to scream, and I wanted to hear all the hearts beating in the stillness.

The program identifies me as a member of Sigma Alpha Mu, something Ken would have found hilarious.

I read our words aloud. The man knew how to live. The twinkle in his eye, the different haircuts—all of them exemplary— the way he could just get away with things, whether it was causing a ruckus at the library or nearly causing you to miss a flight. He was eminently forgivable. He never respected your right to sleep, especially when a new discovery or breakthrough was at stake. The least cynical person on the planet. A big little kid, loyal when it was time to scrap, the reliable collector of inside jokes. Laughter, always.

I've spent years trying to describe that laugh; it was husky and nasal. It scared me that I would one day forget the sound. The way his eyes drooped when he was drunk, his confident smile giving way to a toothy grin. A child's grin. His morning-after rasp, the argumentative tsk-tsks, the coach-like glee when he roused you out of bed, out of your room, into the world.

It was an out-of-body experience. I didn't recognize the words on the page; I was somewhere else. I didn't recognize the clothes I was wearing: the black bowling shirt and pin-striped pants that I'd bought a few days earlier. Each of us must protect our memories of him, I said, because it brought a little bit of him back. It was the only way to bring him with us into the future. I listed all the things we would never do with him, from the long-teased performance of "Piano Man" with Irami and Alec, to giving Steve his birthday present, to graduation, weddings, playing with Gwen's future children. *We're sorry this world is so fucked up. It took you from us, and us from you.*

Sammi had thought the swearing was a bit much for such a grave event.

As I returned to the pews, I felt faint, the week's exhaustion finally catching up to me. For a few seconds, I saw peace. My jaw and shoulders relaxed; I rested my head on Sean's shoulder, draped my other arm around Anthony. The eulogy, built from all our memories, was exactly, at a molecular level, how life felt that day. Maybe it hadn't been a good piece of writing. But it was perfect.

We filed out quietly. It was evening, yet the sun was still out, which I found a little depressing. It was as if no time passed and nothing had happened. I was embarrassed to smoke in front of Ken's family. The underside of my arm burned as I leaned out the window of Sean's Camry, half screaming to everyone in the parking lot that I loved them. We played "Tha Crossroads" at a meaningful volume. It was perfect, too. Delirious and swirly, blissful and sweet, cresting up and down, Bone Thugs-N-Harmony rapping as fast as humanly possible, outrunning time itself, in hopes of catching up to lost friends and family one last time. I'd heard the song hundreds of times before in the dorms, when I'd revolted against its oozing softness. Now it was a sedative, the only music I could bear. Not so much a way of escaping the present as a way of tunneling deeper into its layers and textures for a few minutes. A séance. They were rappers trying their hand at doo-wop, and there was something about the way their voices braided together with a kind of aggressive imperfection. It sounded like proof of something higher.

Everyone was caravanning to Ken's home, where his parents had invited us for a get-together. Sean and I turned out of the parking lot when I realized that I had been here before. The funeral home was just down the street from CD City, where Ken had taken me tape shopping a few months earlier. Sean pulled over so I could smoke a cigarette outside.

His folks ensured that we were all well fed. I couldn't believe that they had the energy to prepare so much food and look after all of us. An unreasonable number of twentysomethings huddled on the family couch. His father's face had a reddish hue, and you could make out where Ken had gotten his eyes from. His parents didn't cry in front of us, but they looked as if they would never laugh again for the rest of their lives. Sean and I took turns going outside and sobbing on the curb. When we left, they said they would mail us any of his things that we wanted to keep.

That night, Paraag, Sean, Dave, and I went to Barona, a casino that Ken often mentioned. It was in Lakeside, about an hour to the east. I didn't want to go, but I also wanted to do something, to go somewhere, to feel the cozy captivity of a car and then wander among people who were strangers to us. We piled into Sean's car, channeling Ken's spirit: "Vegas, baby!" He had been fond of quoting the line from *Swingers* even when the adventure at hand was just a short walk for burritos. Barona was certainly not Las Vegas, at least not the glitzy parts. It felt grimy and sad as people joylessly pulled at levers, asked for their cards with a burned desperation. I lost twenty bucks and spent the next few hours walking in circles, writing about the day's events on the backs of ATM receipts and business cards.

We flew back early on Sunday. When I got to my apartment, I flopped down on the couch, watching dust lazily scatter through the air, and put on a pretty song. I don't remember which one, only that its prettiness, cast against the tranquil blue sky, was unbearable. Once, harmony suggested the possibility of sublime order, of resolutions so eternal and true that we wouldn't merely recognize beauty; we would feel it vibrating through our bodies. Now it just made me feel sick. I kept turning the stereo louder and louder, until it was just a distorted blare, and then I shut it off and went to the bathroom. I took out Anthony's clippers, fitted them with the shortest guard, and shaved off my hair, missing significant patches along the back of my head.

I left to meet Alec and Gwen at a new vegetarian fast-food

restaurant on Telegraph. I walked up Channing, avoiding the sight of Ken's balcony. It felt strange to be alone. Alec and Gwen noted my new haircut, but they were too tired, or kind, to point out how bad it looked. We talked, careful not to say anything.

After lunch, I walked down the street to Amoeba to peruse CDs. But everything reminded me of something, conjured feelings of smallness or brittle shyness that no longer fit. Music no longer modeled a better world. "God Only Knows" unnerved me. I heard all the previous times I had heard it. The scratched-up LP of *Pet Sounds* pulled from Amoeba's used bins, the San Pablo sing-alongs in search of donuts, the study breaks, the scene in *Boogie Nights* that we dissected on the way back from Walnut Creek in Steve's ragtop Jeep. Moments that seem inconsequential until you have a reason to hold on to them, arrange them in a pattern. Carl Wilson no longer sounded tenderhearted and pure, but mocking, keeper of a secret I wanted to know. The majesty of his brother Brian's arrangements, the perfection of the sound, different people coming together inside a beautiful song: it repulsed me. I decided that I could no longer listen to anything from before.

After the funeral, I returned to my summer teaching job in Richmond. The director of the youth center had encouraged me to take some time away, but it seemed wise to resume some routine. Now, during random moments of a math unit, I would launch into monologues about keeping friends close, holding on to the possibilities of youth. "I don't care if I'm older or younger," a ten-year-old named Melissa said in response, "as long as I'm alive." One day, I asked them to make "life maps" that connected their family's journeys to whatever dreams they had for their own future. We watched a VHS copy of the Spice

Girls movie a lot. Whatever energy I could muster day to day was spent praying that the VCR worked. I sat in the back and watched my kids watch their movies, lulled by their capacity to be enchanted. I understood part of teaching is being a vampire. You draw on your students' energies, and you learn just as much as you teach.

I felt a responsibility to keep them safe, even though I didn't understand the particular dangers of their lives. Every moment mattered; every moment was for teaching some life lesson. I spent more time driving them around than marking up their worksheets. After classes ended, I delivered them home, or we ventured to a different, much livelier shopping center down the road. One day, I drove some of them to Blockbuster to rent a movie and then to Target to buy some snacks. I grabbed a pack of baseball cards as I was checking out. One of the girls, a tough thirteen-year-old named Megan, asked if I wasn't too old for baseball cards. I said something to her about the lure of nostalgia, and memories of childhood, and wanting to grasp at those feelings of carefree innocence again. She looked at me and nodded politely, barely disguising her judgment. I was wasting money.

I was driving them around one Friday afternoon; I looked in the rearview mirror and saw four kids on the verge of becoming teenagers, shoulder to shoulder, the kind of intimacy that feels tentative and new at that age. I no longer bothered trying to play them my tapes of underground hip-hop or Sly and the Family Stone, or lecture them on the socioeconomic contexts that had defined their favorite rappers and singers. They wanted to hear 2Pac's hits, not the album tracks. They controlled the radio. A ray of sunshine shot through the car and landed on two of their faces as they sang along to "Nice & Slow." None of them reminded me of myself, or the Asians with whom I'd grown up.

But one of the boys reminded me of Usher; it was in his smile, his posture. The girl next to him looked at him and blushed, self-conscious that her gaze had lingered a nanosecond too long. He just kept swaying from side to side, singing, his tendril-like bangs sashaying, too. These songs were teaching them how to desire, how to express themselves. They were emotions that had yet to take root but would soon overtake them.

That was the year when every other song on the radio featured Master P. At first, this music was too slow. I didn't like the way he leaned into his syllables with such dry extravagance, as though he were rejoicing in how little he had to say. He was moaning, not rapping. I would always point out to my passengers that while Master P was absolutely awful, he was originally from Richmond, just like them. His family-run record label, No Limit, was one of hip-hop's great success stories. They could be entrepreneurs someday, too.

As summer wore on, and I heard "Make 'Em Say Ugh" and Silkk the Shocker's "It Ain't My Fault" more and more, this music made sense to me on a basic, human level. These rappers moved through the world at their own pace. Bodies heave when no words can be found. Sometimes a growl or sob says more. Their beats sounded like death rearranging furniture in the underworld. We drove around so much that all of the songs they loved, from the No Limit anthems to the soft-core slow jams, all of which I'd resisted months earlier, became the sounds I needed the most. The heavenly harps of Brandy and Monica's "The Boy Is Mine," the cooing baby of Aaliyah's "Are You That Somebody?" Music had once taught me about crushes, shyness, the virtues of feeling small. Now I sank into epic, glossy tales of heartbreak and resurrection, songs that indexed lifetimes of triumphs and sorrow, the stakes always greater than any specific boy or girl.

. .

The week after Ken died, my friends and I were inseparable. Sammi, Alec, Gwen, Henry, and I went to see *There's Something About Mary* a few days after we got back from the funeral. As it started, I remembered that Ken and I had seen the trailer for this movie a few months earlier, when we sped to Emeryville for a late showing of *The Truman Show*. We had planned on seeing it together. He was a fresh enough memory that I knew which lines he would have loved, and I could hear him reciting them.

Over time, it became harder to mourn together as we all found ourselves crawling through different stages of sadness, calibrated to our own triggers and intensities. Anthony was back at work on campus when his boss randomly began telling him about how she had survived a mass shooting at a law office in San Francisco in the early 1990s. She didn't explain why she was sharing this story, and he didn't know what to say. But it felt like an attempt to reach out, an adult's hard-won lesson that life goes on. Nobody outside our circle ever knew what to tell us. But at least among ourselves, we understood what silence articulated.

One of the first people beyond the confines of our little world whom I talked to was Jay, my mentee in Richmond. He was a thirteen-year-old with an intense, slightly terrifying smile, and he sat transfixed, taking in every detail of my story. He wasn't in my summer class, but he spent a lot of time at the center, which I took as a good sign. Compared with his quiet, sleepy-eyed brother, Jay was always mouthing off, getting into trouble, and staring down anyone, of any age, who challenged him. I liked having him nearby.

I had promised to take him to the movies. On a quiet Wednesday afternoon, a week and a half after Ken's funeral, I took Jay and some of the other boys from the mentorship program to

Hilltop, the local mall, for a matinee. I was too dazed to realize, until about ten minutes in, that they were far too young for *The Players Club,* a dark comedy about a fledgling strip club. They couldn't believe their luck, squirming and giggling in delight at the first sight of a naked woman.

The movie ended, and we slowly filed out of the theater. Jay looked to me. "Come walk with us in the mall, Hua." I was the chaperone, but he and his friends were protecting me. I told the rest of them what had happened to my friend. "It's hard, man," Saeng, the wisest of the boys, said. His voice cracked a little. "God, that's fucked up." One of them offered to buy me lunch someday.

They never brought it up again. Instead, Jay began carrying my teaching materials for me on the short walk from the youth center to my classroom a few doors down.

In August, during the last week of summer school, the kids challenged the staff to a softball game. This, I thought, would be the perfect way to close the summer. I would redeem my spirit on the diamond.

The big day came, and after a night spent visualizing positive outcomes, I believed things were lining up well. The staff entered the eighth inning trailing by a run, and I was first up. I had played a solid but unspectacular game with a pair of singles and an error-free performance in the field, mostly because few people on either team had played much softball, and everyone kept striking out. This was crunch time and my team needed me.

I was wearing camouflage shorts, a Polo shirt, a Nike visor that had once belonged to Ken, and silver Air Maxes. I hiked my white socks as high as they would go, up to my kneecaps, so as to accentuate my strides as I ran the bases. I took my car keys out of my shorts and handed them to another teacher. I strode to the plate and winked at my students. I tapped the sole of my sneakers with the bat and stepped in. Jay smiled and lobbed the ball my way. I chopped a weak grounder to the right side of the infield. It trickled through the dirt, harmless and impotent. I ran as fast as I could up the line.

The second baseman threw wide, and the ball rolled toward the parking lot. I took a liberal turn at first and arrogantly ran for second. I noticed two outfielders flirting with each other and decided to go for a triple. I imagined a perfect pop-up slide into third, clapping the dust from my hands and seeing a dugout full of cheering administrators. Then I saw the ball, heading toward third, destined to arrive before me. I sized up the third baseman: Megan. She'd been tossing her glove into the air during my at bat, so it's safe to say she was unprepared as the ball and I both headed her way.

I had been searching for direction. This seemed as worthwhile as anything. Run through the green light.

I had committed a lot of good hours to these young people; who would I be to teach them that life is easy or fair, or that one should trust authority? Sometimes, things are fucked up. You take refuge somewhere and realize it's not the dream after all. Cops harass you for no reason; your weary parents' moods seem governed by forces you can't yet name. Your otherwise mild-mannered, twenty-one-year-old mentor comes running at you, absolutely hell-bent on glory. They still had a lot to learn.

The throw to third beat me by a considerable margin, but I slid anyway, crashing into Megan, and kicking at her mitt. The ball popped loose and she went tumbling. My shin was completely torn up; the field was poorly maintained, and the basepaths were lined with rocks and glass shards. I continued on my way, slammed my foot on home plate, and threw my arms in the air. My knee felt cool from all the blood trickling down it. I felt free. I screamed.

None of my teammates—administrators, teachers, other

mentors—greeted me after this most unlikely inside-the-park home run. Rather, they stood there in shock. My boss's mouth was agape; she seemed too terrified to be angry. Another summer school teacher tried to disguise her disgust with a frightened smile. Other adults covered their faces. The boys, delighted, ran over and mobbed me at home.

I felt a sense of relief as the summer ended. Days had piled up; weeks had passed; things had to get better. I wrote about the softball game in my journal and concluded that my new view on things was that "LIFE IS FAST." A gruesome, lunch-meat-sized scab formed on my knee. I appreciated the way it expanded, mutated, took on new crevasses. It looked like a landmass slowly expanding across the sea. I wore the wound like a badge. I loved telling the story of how it happened, because something about the way I reveled in its violence seemed uncharacteristic. And it was also a new story—one that had nothing to do with Ken or the past.

I spent every night at Mira's apartment, but I never felt like talking or doing much of anything. I sulked when we compared class schedules for the fall and realized we would never be able to get lunch together. Her roommate was Charles, one of Ken's little brothers in the frat. He was going out with one of Mira's childhood friends, Kathy. I admired Charles's ritual of ending the day with a beer, a cigarette, and a few innings of baseball on PlayStation. When Mira went to bed, Charles and I played in silence, projecting our fates onto the screen.

Now that my summer job was over, my mom and I flew to Taiwan for a couple weeks to spend time with my father. They thought the change of surroundings would be good for me. It was comforting to settle into such a manageably small, parent-child context. They left me to myself. I had a dream where Ken and I went on a 7-Eleven run and I was relieved that I could give back the Polo Sport shirt that his parents had sent me. The next day, my parents and I went to a temple to make an offering to our ancestors. I had done this hundreds of times before, but this felt different. I wanted to select the best incense stick in the pile; my movements as I approached the altar had to be precise and perfect. As I bowed, I began whispering to him. When I opened my eyes, a fly landed on a string of beads.

A few days after Ken's death, my mom had called my cell phone while I was driving. Sammi answered and they chatted for a few minutes. My mom told her what had happened was horrendous. But we had to find a way to get on with our lives. It seemed like cruel advice, especially since we were still in shock. After that call, my parents and I seldom talked about what had happened.

When we were leaving, my dad gave me a letter he had written on legal paper. "When I look beyond my work," he wrote, "the society, the world frustrate me." He lamented the craven opportunists cheating our economic systems. "We cannot hope the devil will change their minds." My dad never mentioned the events of the previous month, but he wanted to remind me that he and my mom were there for me despite the "uncertainty" of senior year. Maybe I could consider ways to effect change within the legal system, he wrote. "What do you think?"

He also gave me a cassette of Bach's cello suites. "It seems try to touch the subject of 'true freedom,'" he wrote. Maybe I would have a deeper understanding of this than he did. "I still like Beethoven—Brahms—Tchaikovsky—Bartok—Janacek. When I don't feel good, I'll listening those to pacify myself. Of course, Bob Dylan and Neil Young to less extent. How about you?"

· ·

It's weird 'cause we're all growing old without Ken, I wrote in my journal, although by that point he had been gone for only a month. I felt this aching nostalgia for things that happened just hours earlier and wrote them down as a historian might describe a centuries-past crossroads.

The weekend before senior year, I went to Cabo San Lucas with Sammi, Alec, Gwen, Dave, and some others. I stuffed as much as would fit into my backpack. I had taken to wearing the Cuban Sugar Kings cap that Ken had left in my apartment. Alec wore sunglasses the whole time because he had a nasty scar running underneath his right eye. He'd given up sobriety after the funeral. There was an open bar at one of Gwen's work events, and Alec got so drunk that he fell down in the street, cracking his glasses and nearly blinding himself.

I feared our plane to Mexico would crash. That the taxi to the resort would collide with oncoming traffic. That I would contract some rare illness from the bedsheets. That my softball scar would require amputation. One afternoon, everyone else went on a deep-sea fishing trip. Because I couldn't swim, I stayed behind, watching as the boat disappeared beyond the horizon. I walked back and forth on an empty beach, wondering what I would do if something awful happened to them. They weren't fishermen and tour guides; those were criminal masterminds. The sky was gorgeous and calm, but what if a hurricane struck and my friends were stranded? It suddenly made sense to always assume the worst.

We often walked by this one construction site on our way to the beach, and the workers hundreds of feet up would whistle and catcall at Sammi and Gwen. I thought about how generic and normal we must have looked from up there.

Partying in Mexico was the kind of thing I never would have done before Ken's death, but I hoped it would connect me with an openness to fun that honored his memory. I had a fraught relationship with fun. I spent most of my time writing in my journal or smoking outside nightclubs. I was like the death of the party, incapable of switching off, somberly sipping Newcastles, peeling the labels off, and scribbling down the time and location. I constantly admired my scab, picking at it, chiseling at its edges, until it was finally ready to be freed, floating into the warm waters of the Pacific Ocean.

SHUT 'EM DOWN

OU ARE INVOLVED IN PROJECTS OR COALITIONS
ORTING FOLKS ON THE INSIDE, HELPING YOUNG
E STAY OUT, OR STRUGGLING TO CREATE AN
HAUL OF THE WHOLE CRIMINAL INJUSTICE SYS-
- COME TEACH OTHER FOLKS HOW THEY
D BE DOING IT TOO. CONTACT US NOW TO
UP A WORKSHOP OR SPEAK ON A PANEL.

RTICIPATION IS FREE !

PO BOX 339 BERKELEY,
(510)643-2094 (510) 8
WWW.IGC.ORG/JUSTICE/
CRITRESIST@AOL.CO

THERE WAS the passed-down legend of this unassuming engineering major who had gone to our high school, so distraught by his poor showing on a computer science exam that when a would-be mugger approached him with a knife, he grabbed the weapon from his hand, threw it into the bushes, and kept walking. I'm having a bad day, he supposedly said.

Over the course of four years at Berkeley, Sean twice lost a wad of cash to strangers, though the second time was a result of his own gullibility, when a man in a van offered to sell him a brand-new laptop. He showed Sean the box through the window. Two hundred bucks. They went to an ATM together. But as Sean slowly realized this deal was too good to be true, he started to wrestle his money back. The man bit his arm, jumped in his van, and sped off. We couldn't believe that Sean, who'd grown up in New York, or New Jersey, hadn't been more streetwise.

I got jumped for my wallet a few months prior to Ken's party, just down the street from the Rapa-Nui. I was uncertain of the protocol once I gave up the goods. I stood there next to four teenagers as they examined its contents: no money, a Blockbuster card, a fake credit card with the Playboy bunny that had come with the wallet, a pink index card (ideas for a zine), a folded-up picture of Björk. I began running home, and I heard the whooshing of a North Face parka behind me. I looked back and one of the kids was chasing me. He wanted to return my wallet; they felt sorry for me.

None of this made Berkeley seem dangerous, just connected

to a world larger and more complicated than the boring, suburban ones many of us had come from. We didn't go to school in a bubble. College kids will always seem like easy prey to enterprising thieves, and for most students this meant little more than a stolen bike. Ken's murder was a freak occurrence. It was on an entirely different spectrum from the petty, run-of-the-mill crimes the rest of us had experienced. The campus hadn't seen anything like it since the hostage situation in 1990 at Henry's, a bar on Durant Avenue, or the mysterious 1992 stabbing of a student in Eshleman Hall, the campus building that housed the student government and clubs.

The casual danger of a place like Berkeley wasn't tragedy on this scale. It was that the school was so proximate to the world just beyond, there was no real division, and you'd be served bizarre, ugly versions of adult life. Knowledge might not set you free or light your path. It could become a kind of cage.

Grown-up oddballs were always haunting Berkeley's main plaza—sunburned acid casualties, devotees of cause or conspiracy too extreme for a less liberal setting. Some never wore clothes; others seemed perennially overdressed, with heavy coats and posters detailing the connection between Bill Clinton, the CIA, and the Dalai Lama. I occasionally saw an aggressively friendly, middle-aged man on Dwight who dressed in head-to-toe Nazi regalia. The fastidiousness of his outfit underscored his freakishness. You never guessed that a wide-open future might result in a retreat into the most obscure corners of your own mind. The world seemed so simple to them, even if it was unwinnable, a story you told over and over until you mastered it. Maybe that's what made it so simple, their devotion to causes that were forever lost.

An alarmingly muscular man in khakis patrolled the steps of Sproul Plaza in the late afternoons. He paced back and forth, lecturing no one in particular, and from afar it looked as if he were selling workout supplements. But when his homemade posters swung into sight, you realized they were full of ghastly, blown-up images of aborted fetuses. He seemed utterly joyless, bent on provoking rather than persuading us. It was a bit funny imagining the internal monologue of a violently pro-life body-builder. Students tried to engage with him, make him crack, poke around to see if there was anyone home upstairs. But on this day, we didn't want to be reminded about matters of life, death, the underworld. *2 Sept. 1998. The first day, around noon, we were all just sitting on Sproul, listening to all the religious assholes tell us we were going to Hell. Gwen just started bawling. It was hard.*

That fall, the school pieced together a list of Ken's friends and sent us emails offering grief counseling. Therapy seemed exotic and luxurious to me. I wasn't depressed, a condition I associated with a kind of ho-hum stasis. I didn't want to die, even though I was increasingly curious about its logistics. *What was it like on the other side?* I wasn't catatonic or anything. I was busy, frenetic, staying up all night reading and writing.

As far as I knew, none of us took the school up on its offer. At least nobody talked about it. Increasingly, we simply didn't talk about what had happened over the summer. Paraag noted that it had been a pretty good year for many of us until July. Best to figure our own ways forward. I would spill it all to cross-country acquaintances over Instant Messenger and then ignore their phone calls. I sought new routines, a way of resetting my context. My thoughts were always racing back to that night, and it made me feel out of place among my closest friends, who had worked hard to bring some rhythm back to their lives.

I often went down the hall to Paraag and Sean's apartment to watch baseball because they had cable; that was the year Mark McGwire and Sammy Sosa were on a historic race toward

Roger Maris's single-season home run record. I'd stay for a McGwire or Sosa at bat and then quietly go back down the hall. Occasionally, I tagged along to Henry's for two-for-Tuesdays, a cheap beer promotion that was essentially a frat party on neutral grounds. There was often a middle-aged man there on those nights, dressed respectably in a blazer and khakis. He'd go from drinking pensively by himself to buying a round for some fraternity brothers, inserting himself into someone else's glory days. I always zoned out and observed him, wondering when he graduated, whether he was here every night or only Tuesdays, what pleasure he could possibly derive from being around a bunch of sloppy undergrads. He was like an emissary from some alternate time line. Would we be like that in the future? Inevitably, my thoughts spun back to Ken's party, the fact that the bar was just down the block from his frat, all the times we'd hung out at the food court across the street, that mission to smash the windows of the rival house around the corner. It became clear, as my friends downed their beers, that I was somewhere else. Their returns to normal life seemed so easy. I felt left behind and was showy about my sadness. But I also feared their judgment, the possibility that I had stubbornly chosen to stay back.

I wrote Ken about the everyday things he was missing out on: movies, the new recruits to Cal's basketball team, my political theory class, which he would have loved. The professor was a slight, frazzled man named Michael Rogin. I imagined he was what New York was like, nervously pacing, frenetically scribbling out a new cosmos across the chalkboard, dust everywhere, enthusiastically explaining what Nathaniel Hawthorne and Herman Melville had to do with who we were as Americans.

Previously, they had all been the same to me—a bunch of dead white guys. But there was more to it. A chain of interpretations, reinterpretations, and misinterpretations—by readers enthralled by faith, readers who hated what they were forced to read, readers who combed the distant past for glimpses of a future.

Rogin's class was unlike any other I'd taken in the Political Science Department. For one thing, he acknowledged that American history proceeded from conquest and domination. He pointed us toward the repressed currents of guilt or sorrow underlying the nation's greatest works. Everything was subtext. Our nation was haunted by ghosts. After the first day of class, I dashed to his office hours and persuaded him to advise my thesis, even though I had no topic.

Sometimes, Rogin dropped hints about his past. He told us about how he sat next to the Rockefellers at school—those were the days when Harvard made everyone sit alphabetically—and how his classmates had looked down upon him as a working-class Jew. I lived for these brief glimpses. I wanted to understand how he had become a man. I started subscribing to *The Nation* after he mentioned it was his favorite magazine, and I went to Moe's to find all the books he had written on Melville, blackface, Ronald Reagan. I showed up at office hours every week to parrot back things he said in lecture and memorize the books I spied on his desk. I wanted to tell him everything, but I couldn't imagine him caring.

After a couple months, he grew tired of my visiting his office to spitball thesis ideas. "You come here every week," he said, "and you just want to talk." I felt embarrassed; he clearly saw me as a sycophant, not someone whose ideas were worth taking seriously. But he was right. "Come back when you've written something."

. .

There were so many things I wanted to tell Ken. My journal contained my half of our continued conversations: my sputtering relationship with Mira, how Alec and Gwen were doing, the fact that I was hanging out with Ken's frat brother Charles, and that I'd adopted the Padres when we played video games. No room for Wally Joyner, but Quilvio Veras had developed into a decent leadoff batter. The real-life Padres were actually good that year, too. I told him about *The Matrix*, which was the type of movie we would have gone to see on opening night and then stayed up late dissecting over cigarettes, relating it all back to our rhetoric seminars. *Did you see that Baudrillard reference in the first scene?* The movie was about unlearning our relationship to the world. What we considered real life was just a state of permanent dreaming, while our bodies provided sustenance for these incomprehensible machines. I remember thinking, given the choice, would I choose reality or the dulcet ignorance of a dream?

I wanted to impose structure on all that had come before that July night, turning the past into something architectural, a palace of memories to wander at my own leisure. Sammi described us as "looters in a city on fire"; I nicked the phrase for later use. Your consciousness was like a city, and you scavenged and searched for treasured memories of better days. Or maybe memory is more of a fire than a city. It's uncontrollable, fickle, and destructive.

Writing offered a way to live outside the present, skipping over its textures and slowness, converting the present into language, thinking about language rather than being present at all. When one is a student, time is measured in clear increments—the rhythm of the semester, the expanse of summer, which becomes less carefree and more regimented with each passing year. Anticipation draws you through your days—the impending release of a hyped new album, a trailer for a movie that we should see next month. You look forward to the future, even if you can no longer imagine life beyond that morning.

Occasionally, I felt preemptively embarrassed about my private hysterics. *I think the most depressing aspect of keeping a journal is thinking, or knowing, that one day I'll be sitting somewhere reading this. Trying to relive some moments, but struck not by recaptured emotions, rather being struck by how damn deep I tried to sound at some point in the past.*

Some afternoons, I returned to the AOL chat room where Ken, Ben, Sean, and I made fun of the right-wingers. But it felt strange to be on the internet in the daytime. The conservatives-only buddy list we kept for such occasions was largely unpopulated; people like "TruthGator" didn't hang out here during business hours. Without the crowd, egging one another on, the room's temperature was much milder. I chatted with the only person I could find online, a middle-aged woman in the Midwest who never seemed to understand that we were ridiculing her gentle faith in the free market. With few fellow travelers around, she simply wanted to talk about normal things, the patterns of our daily lives, not our respective views on single-payer health care. They were people who felt lonely, searching for teammates who might become friends.

At night, I would retreat to Mira's apartment. We'd sit in silence, sometimes in darkness, eating pizza, our faces illuminated only by the TV. I bristled whenever she would get tickets to go see a show or suggest a movie, ready with some explanation as to why these weren't cool things to do. I brooded when I didn't get my way, though I didn't know what that meant, since I never wanted to do anything.

Our lives were intertwined in such a way that we were always together, which comforted me, even if I lacked the grace to articulate it. Work gave us something to discuss. We were editors for *Hardboiled*, the college Asian American newspaper. At our first meeting of the year, the staff shared story ideas—a retrospective of the Yellow Power movement, the experience of Hmong and Mien kids in the East Bay, sweatshop labor in the Pacific Islands, campus turntablists, the enigma of Asian American conservatives, the subversive politics of lowered Acuras, modified Integras, and street racing. One of the younger editors mentioned that a Japanese American student was murdered over the summer. "Maybe we can look into it," she continued, "and see if it was a hate crime?" *It definitely wasn't a hate crime,* I said. "How can we know . . ." I interrupted her. *It wasn't . . . It was just something fucked up that happened.*

I assumed that Ken had been targeted because he was a college student, not because he was Asian. Maybe the perpetrators saw these identities as interchangeably nonthreatening? But I was mostly upset that my colleague had tried to slot Ken's death into a broader context—one beyond my understanding and control. I was unwilling to relinquish him to some greater cause.

In October, Paraag, Sean, and I were watching Game 1 of the World Series at their place. The Yankees were representing the American League. The San Diego Padres, who'd finished last in their division the year before, cruised through the National League, making their first World Series since 1984. I wondered if I still had the article about Wally Joyner and the charms of his underdog Padres that Ken had written for my zine, the one I was too much of a prick to publish.

It suddenly felt as if my entire faith in higher powers rested on the outcome of this series. Few nonpartisans fancied Ken's Padres. The first game was played in the Bronx, and the Padres led 5–2 going into the bottom of the seventh. Ken had been right all along. They quietly built a quality team, and they had finally come good.

The Yankees rallied in the seventh, eventually tying it 5–5. With the bases loaded and two men out, Tino Martinez stepped in for a 2–2 pitch. Mark Langston of the Padres threw one right down the middle. *Ball.* The replays were damning. The umpire had gotten it completely wrong.

Suddenly Paraag's television felt too big, too overwhelming. The camera panned to the Padres' dugout, full of disbelief, then to the Yankees and their regal, bullying fans, the arc of history suggesting that this was all preordained. I hated every single one of those fans. I wanted them to suffer.

Paraag kept a bottle of Zima on his bookshelf, a shrine built around the last drink that he and Ken never had the chance to share. I glanced at it. It was like a talisman, until it wasn't. Martinez smacked the next pitch into the upper deck. A grand slam.

I humored the possibility that providence was still real, only that it was fickle—that maybe it was some other ghost's chance to taste victory. The Padres never recovered; we could feel the inevitability of the Yankees winning the World Series in that moment. Maybe there was no justice, only randomness, and everything I had endowed with meaning—the flies, the right song on the radio at an unexpected time—was just a coincidence.

Back in July, a couple days after Ken's death, an assistant coach for our college's football team was killed in a bizarre accident. He was camping with a friend when it began to storm. The coach was struck by lightning. While his friend tried to resuscitate him, he was struck by lightning again. It made our world seem so cloistered and spooky that these unusual tragedies occurred so close to each other, reported on adjacent pages of *The Daily Cal.*

Ken's killers were swiftly apprehended. They were identified once investigators followed a string of ATM and credit card transactions throughout Berkeley, Oakland, and Richmond. The perpetrators claimed that their victim was selected randomly and the motive was robbery. When reached for comment, Ken's father told a reporter that he considered his son "a hero. I say that because he gave his life, instead of somebody else's, maybe unknowingly."

What if I had stayed at the party? A question I kept turning over in my mind. Could I have made a difference, or was all of this fated to happen?

I never wondered why they had done it. It was beyond my comprehension. One day, a star from our school's basketball team was walking through the quad when he passed a campus protest to defend affirmative action. A reporter from *The Daily Cal* spotted him and asked him what he thought. The basketball player didn't know what they were protesting but said he was sympathetic to the struggle. "It's fucked up the way it is sometimes," he said vaguely, and it became a worldview that I wrote out over and over in my journal. It was as simple as that. *It's fucked up the way it is sometimes.*

Blame seemed part of some procedural, adult world. Yet I remember gravitating toward the newspaper's grisliest stories for the rest of that year. I wanted to encounter the worst of humanity, to understand larger scales of cruelty and loss. Earlier that summer, a forty-nine-year-old African American man named James Byrd Jr. was walking home from dinner in Jasper, a small town in eastern Texas. Three men in a pickup truck pulled up alongside him. He knew the driver, a young white man named Shawn Berry, who offered him a ride home. Byrd didn't recognize the other two.

Berry drove them to the woods, where his friends John William King and Lawrence Brewer beat Byrd, spray-painted his face, and eventually tied him to the back of their truck. According to autopsy reports, Byrd was still conscious as they dragged him through a field. At some point, he died. They left his body in front of a church and went to a barbecue. All three of them were arrested within days. King and Brewer were involved with white supremacist groups, but people wondered why Berry had taken part. He seemed like a decent kid, with a job at the local movie theater. Later, the people of Jasper said that nobody saw it coming.

That fall, one of the big campus controversies involved David Cash Jr., a Berkeley undergrad who had witnessed his friend Jeremy Strohmeyer assaulting Sherrice Iverson, a seven-year-old African American girl, in 1997, when they were still in high school. Cash and Strohmeyer were at a Nevada casino when Strohmeyer followed Iverson into the bathroom. It's alleged that when Cash walked in on them, Strohmeyer was molesting the girl. He claimed that he asked Strohmeyer to stop but left once things got more violent. Strohmeyer strangled Iverson to death and abandoned her body in the bathroom.

Strohmeyer was convicted, but no charges could be brought up against Cash. According to the letter of the law, he was not an accessory to her murder; he was merely a "bad Samaritan." This is how he ended up with everyone else at Berkeley. The school was powerless to revoke his admission, despite campus protests and petitions demanding his expulsion. What disturbed his classmates wasn't just that he'd done nothing. It was his nonchalance about it. Cash said that he felt no remorse for what had happened. In fact, he was quoted as saying he hoped to get rich by selling his story to the media. How could he feel bad for someone he didn't know—whether it was Iverson or, as he put it, "people in Panama or Africa"? An interviewer from *60 Minutes* asked Cash whether he regretted anything from that night. "I don't feel there is much I could have done differently," he said.

In October 1998, a twenty-one-year-old college student named Matthew Shepard was brutally killed by two men he met at a bar in Laramie, Wyoming. They had offered to give him a ride home, but instead they drove him to an empty field where they tied him to a barbed-wire fence and tortured him. When investigators arrived, Shepard was alive but comatose. His face was caked with blood, save for a trail of tears underneath his eyes. The killers were apprehended a few hours later after getting into a fight with two other men. They denied that the attack on Shepard had anything to do with his sexuality, though one of the killers later tried to invoke a "gay panic" defense, blaming his uncontrollable rage on abuse suffered as a child and his own, buried-deep queerness.

I read about these tragedies carefully, but they didn't bring me any closer to fathoming darkness. I dwelled on all the small moments along the way—what the sky must have looked like just before the succession of lightning strikes, the relief Byrd might have felt when offered a ride home, how a smoky casino smells at four in the morning. Inevitably, I would think about Ken's final minutes, too. What it must have felt like to be locked inside his own trunk. Did he lament those he would leave behind, or was he focused on escape? Trying to understand how these moments could be narrativized after the fact, either in the minds of the perpetrators or in the tales told by lawyers or journalists, was impossible.

I consulted these stories for lessons—versions of grace, or its opposite. I studied the reactions of parents and friends, some merciful, others committed to a more vengeful form of justice. A couple years later, the controversy around Cash's inaction resulted in a new law compelling Nevadans to contact the authorities if they witnessed harm being done to a minor. It became a scenario taught in philosophy classes to debate our ethical and legal obligations to one another as citizens of the world. But at the time, it was a fantasy of what you would do if you ever saw Cash on campus. His stubborn commitment to his own innocence suggested evil's inconceivable depths.

I proposed a thesis on representations of race in American films. The early history of cinematic spectacle, as Professor Rogin often mentioned in class, was a story of racial fantasy, from *The Birth of a Nation* to *The Jazz Singer* to *Gone with the Wind*. For much of American history, the hierarchy that privileged whites over all others was encoded in law. And while the end of legal segregation brought opportunity to many, the logic of white supremacy remained, manifesting itself in ways that were furtive, almost invisible. There were still moments of racial terror. But in the post–civil rights era—with its mantra of color blindness—racism was no longer believed to be an institutional reality. This was the larger fiction that all the smaller ones served.

I spent a lot of time shuttling between my apartment and a Blockbuster down the street. I wasn't renting and watching movies, I clarified to anyone who bothered asking about my thesis: I was exploring the cinematic imagination. I was analyzing *narrative,* not stories. I lived in that subtext-mining mode that Ken and I perfected, only now I was doing it in broad daylight, as a serious intellectual pursuit, rather than late at night.

I sought a state of constant occupation. In September, Berkeley hosted an international conference on the prison-industrial complex, a concept that many of us were learning for the first time. Angela Davis was one of the conference's organizers. Hundreds of activists, scholars, and artists were coming to campus to explore the relationship between the boom in prison construction, the militarization of policing, and the criminalization of Black and brown communities. I volunteered to put flyers up around town.

The morning of the conference, another volunteer lamented that Tupac was no longer around, because he surely would have come to something like this. I thought the same of Ken, who always attended my panels. I registered visitors and showed speakers to their rooms. Eventually, I found myself in a room for Asian American leftists discussing our role in this struggle. Someone began decrying an ideology called "neoliberalism," which confused me, because I didn't know what the term meant. I assumed this was just a new and better version of liberalism, which didn't sound that bad. Brochures were passed around detailing the plights of Asian American prisoners like Jay Siripongs, Yu Kikumura, and David Wong. I began writing them letters, asking whether I could interview them for my zine.

In November, I saw a flyer for a program to tutor inmates at San Quentin State Prison. I wasn't very good at teaching teenagers; maybe I would fare better with adults. Mira and I went to an info session, and a background check later we were carpooling to the prison, which was about ten minutes past the Richmond Youth Project, just on the other side of the bay. Our relationship had settled into a stasis. "Let's make the most of the time we have together," she said that winter.

Every few weeks, I brought Rogin a ten-page essay parsing the narrative tropes of America's cinematic imagination. He encouraged me to apply to graduate school in any field but political science. He suggested New York University, and it became my dream. I constantly talked about going to New York, when my life would properly begin anew. Mira said she was excited for me, rarely asking what my move would mean for us.

At San Quentin, there were only three rules. Guards searched our bags on the way in and out, so we could bring only sanctioned books and papers. We were prohibited from wearing the color blue. If we did so by mistake, the guards issued us white jumpsuits. The inmates all wore blue, and the tower guards needed to be able to distinguish us, just in case. Finally, under no conditions were we to run in the courtyard. This, too, was for the tower guards. Otherwise, we could shake hands with our students, talk to them about the outside world, sit close enough to see chipped teeth, pockmarks, spots missed while shaving. We could lean in and whisper about dreams and nightmares.

We met with them in the evenings. I was assigned Lefty and Sean, who were both taking a class on American politics. Lefty was soft-spoken, with a carefully groomed mustache. He seemed gentle to a fault. "I just have one question," he said one day. "What's pizza like now?" Had we, as a society, come up with new toppings, new shapes? He was awestruck when I described the concept of a stuffed crust and revolted by the thought of "dessert pizza." Sean was boisterous with broad shoulders. His gold-rimmed glasses looked like part of a disguise. He claimed to be part of a very famous crime family in the Boston area that I didn't know anything about. If I ever found myself there, he said, let him know. He could recommend some great places to eat.

Our classroom had a chalkboard, movable tables, a computer, and shelves full of reference materials. I started working with a Puerto Rican named Jimmy who always seemed dazed. He missed his daughter, and he wished to be anywhere but there.

Jimmy often told me about growing up in Los Angeles in the 1970s. Once, when he was a teenager, he snuck into a recording studio in Hollywood. He came upon Stevie Wonder, who was working on *Songs in the Key of Life.* The memory—jarred loose when I told him that I spent a lot of time at record stores— transported him. Jimmy told me to go find this album. Many things would make sense afterward. But I wasn't ready for beautiful music. *Maybe the idea of harmony doesn't seem right,* I wrote to Ken, recounting what Jimmy had told me. *Symmetry and grace hurt more these days.*

Eventually, I started working with Viet Mike—the nickname distinguished him from the other Mike, who was Black—and Eddy. Eddy was Chinese American. I couldn't tell if he was my age or ten years older than me. He had sharp cheekbones and lie-detector eyes, the stocky build of someone who spent a lot of his free time doing push-ups. He was quiet and polite.

Nobody ever talked about what they'd done to end up here, and you were never to ask. Eddy simply told me he had done something regrettable and that he was working hard to pay back his debt. When his family arrived from China, his father had worked at Burger King. "He only needed to know three things," Eddy said. "Lettuce, cheese, mayonnaise." Eddy was busy running the streets with his friends, living out his Chow Yun-Fat gangster fantasies. That night, I wrote Ken about something Eddy had shared with me: *He had never told his dad he loved him until going to San Quentin, and he had never heard the words from his dad, either. Going into the pen, though, he realized (this part he switched into Chinese) that he may die at any time.*

You could never predict how each night at San Quentin would go. Sometimes, we would be sent back home as soon as we arrived; there was a lockdown and classes were canceled. Other times, we showed up, and it took the students a few minutes to adjust to our presence because of something that had happened to them at dinner; you couldn't move beyond simple pleasantries. Awkward moments reminded us of the context of our encounter. Were they as bad as the most heinous acts they had committed? A reading on political institutions would spill into a strange reverie about who they once were. "I studied architecture at night," one of the students told me. "I loved to get high. Do some speed and just sit and watch the buildings. The bus is our world. The windows, piss, vomit, how we carelessly take advantage of this thing which exists to help us."

At the end of each night, we gathered in a courtyard to say our goodbyes. It was peaceful. Our students' dark blue uniforms dissolved into the darkness. I spoke to Eddy in Chinese, and he responded in English. It was okay to do this in the classroom, he whispered, but it made the guards out here uncomfortable if we spoke in a language they couldn't understand.

I felt safe; I hadn't felt that way in a while. I looked up at the sky and thought about how it would look later that night, when I was smoking on my balcony. *I'm scared,* I wrote Ken. I no longer felt *linear progress.* The only progress, I continued, *occurs on paper, as words and lines accumulate,* as paragraphs became pages. *Maybe someday there will be insufficient disk space.*

That December, it was time once again for the Secret Non-Denominational Winter Holiday Gift Giver. We agreed to chip in and send Ken's family something. A fancy cheesecake—his favorite dessert.

Mira was home in Los Angeles for the holiday. She told me she wasn't sure our relationship was still working. She was no longer happy. I pleaded with her to take a few days to think about it, drawing on all the highs and lows we had shared together. Was I ever happy? I couldn't say. We agreed to try harder once we were back at school in a few weeks.

He would have turned twenty-one that Christmas Eve. He always griped about how his birthday never felt special, since everybody was already celebrating anyway. I was back in Cupertino for winter break. I drove to a local park to smoke a cigarette and then went to Safeway to buy a six-pack of Newcastle Brown Ale and ingredients to bake a birthday cake.

I had a dream about Ken. Whenever this happened, it would flash by so quickly that I would wake up in tears. But on this occasion, I stayed dreaming a little longer than usual. *I've changed so much, since . . . or rather because . . .* , I said to him. But he stopped me and just grinned. I know, he replied. He even coaxed me into admitting that I had gone out and bought a Pearl Jam CD in his absence. I woke up smiling.

. . .

Once I told Eddy what had happened. It never occurred to me on any conscious level that I was in search of anything at San Quentin—that the perpetrators might be inside here somewhere. Eddy listened intently and shook his head. It was a real shame. He reminded me that he and the other men in the college program were, on the whole, penitent about their pasts. But that didn't describe everyone in here.

The more we heard about the night of Ken's death, the more utterly random and improbable it all seemed. His killers left a trail of obvious clues, and their general sloppiness felt cruel. If we were going to lose him, let it be at the hands of a mastermind, someone worth the full force of our hatred.

The arraignment was in April. Ken's parents came up from San Diego. I went with Alec, Sammi, Gwen, and some other friends. As we entered the court building, Alec was shown through the wrong door, and he stood just a few feet away from one of Ken's killers. He would replay that moment in his mind for years, spinning a maniacal revenge fantasy all different ways. We filed into the courtroom and took seats in the back. The defendants looked vacant and desiccated as they shuffled in. The man was small with an unkempt Afro; he kept staring off into the distance. His girlfriend seemed as though she hadn't slept for weeks. They were dressed in baggy tan uniforms. It was unreal that they had the power to take a life. The one who had pulled the trigger looked shorter than me. The judge read the charges with a bureaucratic flatness. The entire hearing took a few minutes. The court would reconvene in a few months. The local newspaper reported that someone related to one of the perpetrators began apologizing to Ken's parents in the parking lot outside the courthouse.

The arraignment was the same week as the Columbine massacre. I remember reading all sorts of articles trying to grasp why the Columbine killers had done it, retracing their steps, reckoning with where it had all gone wrong for them. Was it the fault of video games, Hollywood, high school bullying? But I didn't understand the point in offering them the privilege of narrative. I was more fixated on the paths that had come to an end.

A reporter visited the apartment complex where Ken's alleged killers lived. It had never occurred to me to learn more about them. It wasn't until reading about them later that I realized they were around our age. They were twenty-three and nineteen. Alec and I wondered whether they would get the death penalty. Whether I still objected to capital punishment. I wondered in my journal if death was worse than *the knowledge that the world continues outside.*

When the reporter asked neighbors in the complex about the couple, many of them expressed surprise. The owner of their unit recalled a young man who loved rap music and going to church on Sundays. He had plans to enroll in trade school, and he would lobby the neighbors to ensure that the "wrong element" never moved into their building. "In all the dealings I had with him, he was kind and polite," the owner explained. "I genuinely liked him."

I remember one of the last times I went to San Quentin. It was spring, a few weeks after the Roots released *Things Fall Apart.* Mira and I drove together even though she'd recently broken up with me. She had tired of my mopey negativity, the way I looked past her toward some future in New York. I was sad, though I knew she was right. I was a leech; I needed comfort and stability, and I gave nothing back. There was no dramatic betrayal, just a relationship that had run its course. We were still committed to the student paper and our work at the prison, so we did our best to remain friends.

As we crossed the bridge, a ray of light shone through the clouds—the prison looked iridescent. It was the kind of scene I had wanted to see for months, a clue that beauty was still possible. Maybe it was nothing more than shifting cloud patterns. But I saw it.

I had snuck a mixtape into San Quentin a few weeks earlier and slipped it to Mike (the Black one), who said he'd share it with others. Public Enemy, Bad Brains, Sly and the Family Stone, stormy compositions by Max Roach and Charles Mingus that I'd recently discovered in Amoeba's jazz aisles. Mike told me he'd listened to the tape. He grinned. "It was really . . ." He paused. "The music was really *hard*." I had never noticed his green eyes or the freckled softness of his cheeks when he smiled.

I exchanged addresses with my students. A disarmingly gentle one gave me a peppermint that he had saved from dinner. He said that I had helped him feel human again. Eddy handed me an envelope with my name written in loopy cursive. Inside was a bracelet made of tiny green and yellow beads that he had crafted for me.

"It's kinda hard with you not around." It was a lyric from "I'll Be Missing You," a song that Puff Daddy, Faith Evans, and 112 released in 1997 as a tribute to the Notorious B.I.G., who had been shot dead at an intersection in Los Angeles earlier that year. I kept repeating it to myself. Puff was an avatar of gloss and superficiality, and the song was corny and smothering. But that's what drew me in. The strange hedge of "kinda," the euphemism of "not around." The not-quite singing and mumbled raps. Puff, so exaggerated and larger than life, becoming flesh and bones. Faith, who knew Biggie in ways Puff did not, trying to soar above it all. It came to seem like it had been made for me, even if it was clearly not. I only wanted to hear songs like these, and hip-hop was filled with friends plotting and scheming, complimenting and complementing each other, conquering the world together, carrying one another's weight.

"I'll Be Missing You" posed a series of questions and scenarios to turn over in my head. Would Puff, as the song claimed, actually give it all away for Biggie to come back? What did it mean to represent for another, to bring them with you on your adventure? Would they one day be replaced by the character you invented in tribute? Maybe he just wanted to keep him around until he understood how to properly mourn him. To keep him around, a living memory, until he was ready to move forward, alone. Not raising the dead so much as singing along to an echo.

Professor Rogin was pleased with my thesis, maybe because the entire thing was an attempt at mimicking his style. The wild juxtapositions, the frantic rhythm, the rhetorical feints, the fire-and-brimstone conclusions. He had taught me a different relationship to culture. I'd never been interested in the distant past. But now I recognized that you could use history for your own end. My thesis was essentially a collection of long reviews looking at how recent movies like *He Got Game, Rush Hour,* or *Smoke Signals* dealt with race. Even though racial domination remained inescapable, these films offered retreat into your own imagination, the strength of your will, the salvation of friendship and shared struggle. The thesis was an escape as well as a tribute, a way of extending a series of unfinished conversations. I had done it all for a reason to write out my acknowledgments. I thanked Ken, and I remember feeling as though he were real again as I typed out his full name. I speculated that the as-yet-unfinished film *Barry Gordy's IMBROGLIO* would someday enact many of my work's critical insights.

I was actually happy today, I wrote in my journal that spring. *I mean bullshit happy, that lighthearted feeling of carefree dizziness.* The impetus for my joy was a slick play during a Cal basketball game. *I really hope you can read this. I don't care if you can see through me,* I wrote, confessing to a list of imperfections and insecurities. *Just as long as you can see me.*

WAS AT A RECORD STORE in San Francisco, a year to the day after Ken's passing. The owner was sorting through new arrivals, when he coolly chuckled to himself and held up a copy of *The Last Dragon* soundtrack. "Remember this?"

I searched his face for a clue of some kind. This wasn't a rare record, though I had never seen it before. I just stared at him, waiting to hear Ken's laugh. "It was a movie from the '80s," he explained, pricing it and sliding it back into the bin. *I know it,* I finally said, and I began trying to explain how bizarre it was to see this LP on this particular day. I told him about my friend, the time we stayed up late watching *The Last Dragon,* our conviction that Bruce LeeRoy shed light on deeper mysteries about race, America, ourselves. *I've been searching . . . ,* I continued, and he added it to my pile and said I could take it for free.

That night, I stayed up until sunrise making an issue of my zine. "A year ago at this precise moment I was on my way home from a rave," I wrote on the first page. There were record reviews and short riffs on identity, an essay by Eddy about life at San Quentin, excerpts from a paper I'd written for class about indigenous rituals of gift giving, and the "delayed reciprocity" that gave meaning to graffiti. I finally published Ken's essay about Wally Joyner and the Padres. On the last page, I recounted that night, blacking out his name each time it appeared. "What an embarrassment I will always pine for," I wrote, imagining what might have happened if we had gone swing dancing. "To make ▉▉ topple over in laughter."

. .

Near the end of senior year, I started dating Joie. There are people who try to cheer you up when you're sad, and those who try to join you wherever you are. Her instinct was always to follow me down.

She was also a political science major, though we'd never taken any of the same classes. I was enchanted by the way she moved through the world, taking in as much of it as possible, holding her body with purpose and intention, something I attributed to her background in dance. Her hair was big and curly, aura-like. I wanted to get lost inside her.

Joie listened as I told her stories about Ken; she'd read about what happened in the school paper, but never met him. I recounted every mundane detail of him to her. She told me about her family, their struggles after leaving Korea, the tribe of unbreakable women that she was a part of. She was from San Jose, not too far from where I'd grown up. But unlike me, she'd had to fight for everything she achieved. Now she, too, dreamed of going to New York for graduate school. Maybe we would end up there together.

I'd never been around someone with such a lust for life, an appreciation for its exultant highs as well as its darkest lows. I'd also never done drugs before. She patiently taught me how to use a bong, after which I knew she would make a brilliant, inspiring professor someday. I hadn't known that rolling a joint for someone else could communicate such compassion and deep care. She made me feel as if I could understand impossible things.

Joie got into NYU for graduate school, but I did not. I ended up going to Harvard. Boston had been Ken's dream, not mine. In theory, I would be studying all the foundational things about

American history and literature that I had ignored until college was nearly over. I was ignoring them still. Cambridge was not Berkeley, and there were certain shades of gold and orange that I now urgently missed. Instead of studying, I searched the names of the dead on the internet. Rather than writing seminar papers, I would stay up until dawn trying to describe a bass line or a synthesizer ("like jet-exhaust"), not because I was transfixed with the sound itself, but because I needed to perfect my skills of description. I spent most of my first year at Harvard looking forward to bus rides to visit Joie in New York.

I was at a party in Williamsburg, sometime in the weeks after 9/11, when nighttime in the city was still a mix of nasty fumes and desperate euphoria. Sammi had moved back to New York, and Gwen was visiting. I was sitting on Sammi's bed, rolling a joint, and Gwen asked me, were you and Ken really that close?

We weren't stoned yet, and within a few minutes maybe this conversation wouldn't matter at all. But I panicked. I didn't know what to say. I remembered the intensity of Gwen's heart-break during our last year at Berkeley, how difficult it became for us to talk about anything else and then, eventually, anything at all. How strange it was that she had to continue living at the Rapa-Nui for the rest of the year. To her, he was "Kenny." They shared a closeness unique to friendships between young men and women. I knew that he was a sweet and vulnerable person, but she understood these qualities in a way that I never could.

Maybe I misremembered a lot along the way. Or a little thing was replayed in my mind so often that it hardened into the memory of having once been routine. I knew she was wrong— that our friendship was staged in private, on balconies, in cars, walking in search of pizza. But how could I ever be sure?

Everyone else eventually passed out. I lay there staring at the network of exposed pipes along the ceiling—something you rarely saw back in California, a period of life that suddenly felt like the ancient past. What she said cast a pall over my memories, my ability to tell a story about myself. Maybe Ken had tired of me and once mentioned this to her.

I spent most of my time as a PhD student shopping for used books and records, secondhand clothes, old magazines. I was assigned an essay by the philosopher Walter Benjamin about the aura that emanates from a work of art. One is conscious of a painting's singularity in the world; you can situate it in a time and place. You're always aware of its provenance, not just that the painter's hand touched this years ago, but that the painting itself has passed through even more hands over time, beheld by a string of previous owners. This part, rather than Benjamin's belief that all of this had something to do with fascism, stayed with me. I thought I was encountering a lesser, probably debased, version of the aura while sifting through old, vintage things, connecting me to some anonymous listener or reader of the past. How did they hear this piece of music? Inspect the grooves: What song did they play more than others? Why did they underline this sentence and not that one?

I was always thinking about the past, pursuing other people's memories and dashed dreams. The aspect of my course work I loved was the archival research, snooping through boxes of old files, looking for ways to access some deeper understanding of someone's art. I was fascinated by the kinds of stories you could tell with the things someone left behind. An obscure, experimental novelist's personal files containing a brochure for a yacht. Was this his true dream, or material for satire, an ethnographic specimen detailing what normal people coveted?

Joie and I found grad school vexing. It was hard to wrap our heads around the fact that we were beginning a process that would take seven or eight years. Would we shuttle between Boston and New York for that long? We lived for immediate pleasures—cheeseburgers and whiskey, drugs and sex, bubbling pots of kimchi stew, throwing up on sidewalks, the world-conquering thrill of finally hailing a cab outside the club. I was in school because it was a kind of holding pattern, drifting toward some vague horizon. But her past still lingered. Whenever she told me stories about her family, her traumas, she always held some of it back. Early on, she'd told me I would never truly understand. We were in new cities, losing ourselves to new excesses, finding our way to higher rooftops, seeing a different shade of sunrise. But we were escaping different things. I wasn't mailing portions of my grad stipend back home to help my mom.

A few months into graduate school, we took ecstasy on the banks of the Charles River—an alternative to serious discussion of tomorrow. Might as well be present, at least for now. Nothing happened at first. "The drugs don't work," I joked, the title of a song by the Verve that I'd liked in college.

But then I looked at the Charles and it was no longer a river. There was no water, just an endless run of silver marbles rolling in slow motion. I laughed, and my body expanded to the ends of the universe. Any sensation lingered and rippled forever; there was no border between our skin and the Cambridge humidity. The drugs did work.

I never listened to the Verve anymore. Their music reminded me of the fall of 1997, when Ken, Sean, Ben, and I would play their CDs while we crashed right-wing chat rooms. But remembering the song title returned me to a line about "a cat in a bag / waiting to drown" that always made me think of Ken's final minutes, trapped in the trunk of his own car. I was sinking into the moment. I chewed my gum faster and faster. I tried looking directly at the sun to wipe my mind clean.

We walked back to my room. For a while, we lay on my twin bed in silence, unable to move. The room throbbed with each breath. She got up and walked to my stereo, which was just a few feet away. It seemed to take an hour for her to make her way there. She flipped through my CDs. Whatever you do, I said, please don't play "The Drugs Don't Work." I couldn't bear it right now. She looked at me from across the room, then down at her reflection in the CD. When she pressed play, she looked at me again, despondent and deserted, as though she couldn't help it.

For days, I couldn't shake a feeling of despair, and I was scared by the fact that some confluence of memory, song, and person could make me feel that way. I maintained belief that the lows were just a price paid to feel such highs again. But she struggled to imagine a future together, at least one that would satisfy the kind of conformist, middle-class telos that had produced me. We had a journal that we shared, and we would trade it back and forth every time we saw each other, entrusting it with our deepest sorrows and fears, writing down things that were too difficult to say, interweaving our respective reasons for sadness, trying in vain to co-author a common story into existence, until this was no longer possible.

Late at night, when I needed a distraction from my studies, I examined the contents of the padded envelope where I kept various Ken-related things. A pack of Export As with two ciga-rettes left. The funeral program. Itineraries, a boarding pass, a map of San Diego. Punch lines written on napkins. Some pages from *Barry Gordy's IMBROGLIO,* a copy of a letter I'd sent to Ken's parents, cassette tapes. A receipt for a journal, a black shirt, and pin-striped pants.

A paperback copy of Edward Hallett Carr's *What Is History?* with the USED sticker across the spine. We were buying our textbooks when Ken saw it assigned for another class. It looked provocative enough, so he added it to his cart. I remember him reading it that night instead of whatever his professor had assigned. He handed it to me when he was done—"You'd be into this." I read the description on the back. *This is all basic stuff, right?* I said to him. I passed off something I once heard someone say about Hegel. *We know this already, right?* History is a tale we tell, not a perfect account of reality, I continued. You just have to figure out whether you trust the storyteller.

He left the book at my apartment, in case I ever deigned to actually read it. Carr published *What Is History?* in 1961. He served as a diplomat for many years before pursuing a life in academia, where he published a series of influential works on international relations. *What Is History?* began as a series of lectures he delivered at Cambridge. "When we attempt to answer the question, What is history?, our answer, consciously or unconsciously, reflects our own position in time"—as well as the future we hope to see. Carr believed in approaching the historian's words with some skepticism. The facts of the past are largely indisputable—what day something happened, the signatories of a treaty, who was in the battalion when the siege began. But how these facts are arranged suggests "an unending dialogue between the present and the past."

The story we assemble from those facts is unsettled. The animating forces of history, the intentions and motives, the chicanery and deceit—much of it results from interpretation. "No document can tell us more than what the author of the document thought—what he thought had happened, what he thought ought to happen or would happen, or perhaps only what he wanted others to think he thought. None of this means anything until the historian has got to work on it and deciphered it." Over time, the historian's judgments assume the appearance of unassailable, empirical truth. To understand the past, we must reckon with the historian's own entanglements, the way past, present, and future remain forever "linked together in the endless chain of history."

When I finally opened Ken's copy of this book, years later, in my Boston apartment, I realized he had read it closely, underlining passages that moved him, taking notes and writing responses in the margins.

Later at night, when the vulnerability of total exhaustion set in, I tried writing scenes from our past. I struggled to describe the simple things, like the dry music of his laugh, the bemused look he'd give just before he trapped you into contradicting yourself. I couldn't remember how tall he was, whether he wore derbies or Timberlands. The more I wrote about Ken, the more he became someone else.

I still felt awful about leaving early that night. But now these feelings drifted elsewhere, toward the possibility that I was telling a story that flattered the narrator, forcing grace and intention onto every stray memory. A self-consciousness that everything was combed for meaning, where friendship's casual rhythms rarely warranted this kind of scrutiny. A creeping shame that I once wondered if he thought about us in his dying moments, as if he had been able to think at all. When the only truth is that it's fucked up the way it is sometimes.

I searched the internet for Ken, even though he had stopped generating content years before, and whatever version of the web we had used in our teens was long since gone. Back then, browsers were just directories, rather than layers of sedimented knowledge, preferences, data-mined keystrokes. The appeal was that it was ephemeral and labyrinthine, a web that dissolved, rather than a physical net. A series of unconnected wormholes.

I was looking to see if anyone had kept his name alive. At first, scraps from local newspapers reporting on the trial showed up, announcements from his local church about the scholarship set up in his honor. But shards of the past kept disappearing, crowded out by algorithmically preferred results. More people with his name began to emerge. A political scientist in Japan. A guy with a start-up. Our generation didn't leave a broad enough footprint. I read that his parents had continued contributing to Berkeley's alumni fund, even though their son never had the chance to graduate. Instead, Ken became a data point in a *Daily Cal* article about violence at Berkeley, a way of connecting the early 1990s hostage crisis at Henry's to a freak stabbing of an engineering student in 2008. He offered context.

I never looked up the perpetrators. But one night, my searches landed me on a website for people trying to erase DUIs from their driving records. It was like a relic of the old internet, where pages were populated with placeholder dummy text. The company had acquired thousands of pages of legal documents and were using them to build a seemingly useless database.

The web page reprinted an appeal filed by one of the assailants. It was another version of a story I'd played out in my mind countless times, but never from the other perspective.

On the evening of July 18, 1998, the text recounts, Kenneth I—— threw a housewarming party at the Rapa-Nui, a building on the corner of Channing and Fulton.

As things were getting started at I———'s, a young couple from Vallejo took a BART train to Berkeley. At the station, they met a man who was about twenty years older than them. He told them about a party just off campus. They walked by to check it out, but it was still early, just a few people mingling on a balcony. So the three of them went to the movies. Afterward, they explored Berkeley. The two men walked ahead of the woman, who couldn't hear what they were talking about.

At around 3:00 a.m., they returned to the party. The older man hid around the corner, while the couple waited in the garage. When I——— came down the stairs, the man pointed a gun at him. He told I——— to open the trunk of his car and get inside. They took his shoes. The woman drove I———'s 1991 Civic around the corner to where the older man was waiting. He took the keys from her and began driving. At one point, the police pulled up alongside them and then kept going. The older man pulled over. He got scared and asked the woman to get behind the wheel instead. After a few minutes, they switched back, after her boyfriend complained about her driving.

Eventually, they ended up at some warehouses north of Berkeley. The men took I——— out of the trunk. They were gone for about five minutes. The younger man returned I——— to the trunk, and they drove to an ATM, where they withdrew three hundred dollars. While the woman waited, she heard I———'s muffled voice. He asked if he could have his shoes back. She didn't respond.

Afterward, they drove to a gas station, where the two men got out and talked. The older man left. The young couple drove to Vallejo, where they ended up at an empty lot on York Street. The woman watched as her boyfriend took I——— out of the trunk. She looked away as they walked a few steps into an alley. She heard two shots. Her boyfriend returned.

They drove away, saying nothing to each other about what just happened. They parked I——'s car on the lawn in front of their apartment.

A fisherman came across I——'s body at 5:30 a.m., not that long after he'd been left for dead.

That Sunday, the nineteenth, the couple went to the mall with some of their friends, where they charged a couple thousand dollars' worth of things to I——'s credit card. They told their friends that they had a long night. That they'd had to do a Bonnie and Clyde on someone. That person was now gone. He had begged for his life.

The police staked out the young couple's apartment and, upon serving them with a warrant, found I——'s things as well as the murder weapon. They picked up the older man, too. At one point, in the initial report, a detective asked the defendants about "the Asian kid," and it took me a moment to realize they were talking about Ken.

The woman is reported to have shown little remorse in the moment, or in the days after. The authorities eavesdropped as she talked to her friends on the phone, maintaining her innocence, fretting the state of her nails. She later claimed that there was something off about her boyfriend that night. He'd always been so mild-mannered. I had heard him rap along to violent songs, she said, but that wasn't who he was. She was scared by all the things she had seen him do. He hadn't taken his medicine, she said, without fully elaborating. This had concerned her. She couldn't tell what was going on in his head.

A couple years after Ken's murder, I sat on the moonlit steps of Sproul Plaza with Alec, who was tending bar in Berkeley. How much of the confusion surrounding our paths was generic postcollege stuff, and how much of it owed to how our lives had been recalibrated around these new scales of fear and failure? At nights, on his way home from work, Alec carried a machete in his backpack. We leaned back and stared at the sky, and he said something about being very tired. We were twenty-two, maybe twenty-three. I was back in the Bay Area during a holiday break from grad school. *Two years later (almost) it makes sense,* I wrote that night, *though it has seamlessly become part of everything we do. We both agreed that the hardest part will come years, perhaps a decade down the road.*

Edward Hallett Carr hoped that *What Is History?* would help light a way forward. He died in 1982, six years before the birth of his great-granddaughter, Helen. She became a historian herself, engaging in a lifelong "imagined dialogue" with her great-grandfather about the nature of their work.

I always felt as if I were reading *What Is History?* alongside Ken. I imagined the moments where we would agree, his practical-minded sense of the world colliding with my contrarian radicalism. I delighted when he underlined the same passages as I would have, and not the obvious thesis statements, but Carr's playful digressions. Some of those sentences felt as though they were tethering different planes together. "Only the future can provide the key to the interpretation of the past; and it is only in this sense that we can speak of an ultimate objectivity in history. It is at once the justification and the explanation of history that the past throws light on the future, and the future throws light on the past." We were on opposite ends of Carr's thought, Ken in the past, me in the future.

One underlined passage about the role of the accident in history captivated both of us. "Nothing in history is inevitable except in the formal sense that, for it to have happened otherwise, the antecedent causes would have had to be different." We consider the various options and identify the missteps, when in reality these alternative paths were never open. What happened simply happened, and to poeticize all that never transpired leads us somewhere else—not history, but faith. It doesn't help us understand the future, only our investment in the past. "As a historian, I am perfectly prepared to do without 'inevitable,' 'unavoidable,' 'inescapable,' and even 'ineluctable.' Life will be drabber. But let us leave them to poets and metaphysicians."

Maybe everything isn't a clue. For a while, I wanted to know what movie they had seen that night, which songs his killer loved rapping along to, what other parties were going on in Berkeley that night, whether any music was playing in Ken's car when they keyed the ignition, what they bought the next day. All of these minuscule, knowable facts, because they couldn't possibly explain why they had done it. No context made their actions "inevitable" or "unavoidable."

But sifting through these small moments of the past was a way of resisting the future. On the last page of his book, Carr addresses professional colleagues and their attempts to turn history into some kind of science. He looks out upon "a world in tumult and a world in travail." Somehow, he remains optimistic. There's no other way to be. The only constant in this life, in this work, is the passage of time, and with it, change. "And yet," Carr writes, quoting Galileo, and beholding our world, "it moves." Underneath the book's final sentences are two additional words. I recognize the compressed squiggle, the smudged red ink of his ballpoint pen, but whatever Ken has added remains illegible to me.

. . .

I went to visit Ken once at his job at Nordstrom. He used to tell me stories about selling children's shoes, all the different families that would come in, which ones he'd look out for, the overbearing ones he'd treat with an inscrutable terseness.

The rush just before graduation, and the subsequent hail of sheepish returns just after graduation. I found these people uninteresting—they were too old and too young—so I found the stories uninteresting. But I listened politely.

One day, I was in San Francisco, and I told Ken I'd come find him and we could ride BART back together. Out of principle, I never shopped in department stores or malls. I had no idea that children's shoes weren't just next to adult shoes, and I got lost. I was already running late; I didn't have time to find a pay phone and page him.

When I finally found the children's wing, I saw the shoes, but I didn't see Ken, and I assumed he'd already gotten off work and returned to Berkeley. There was a family waiting at the register. I was standing at an angle where I could see Ken coming out from the storeroom in the back, carefully tying a balloon around his finger. When he finished, he looked at the loop, then at the balloon, just above his head, safely anchored to his finger, and smiled a goofy smile. He reappeared at the counter and handed it to the little boy waiting with his parents, and the child smiled an even goofier smile.

Then Ken looked up, saw me, and smiled again.

When you're young, you do so many things hoping to be noticed. The way you dress or stand, the music played loud enough to catch the attention of another person who might know a song, too. And then there are things you do as you step out into the world, the real world full of strange adults, testing out what it means to be generous or thoughtful. In that instant, before every memory was placed along some narrative arc, before the act of remembering took on a desperate air, I simply felt lucky to witness something so effortlessly kind—to see my friend do something that was good.

· ·

My second year of graduate school, I moved into an old house down by the Charles River. My roommate Brian's birthday was July 19, the date Ken died, which felt significant. I went to a lot of baseball games, hoping to glimpse a specter haunting the wrong time line, a Japanese American law school student heaving peanuts through the muggy Boston air. I would show up at a class I was teaching and look around, hoping to see us.

One day, I realized that seemingly everyone in my PhD program had availed themselves of the free semester of therapy that our graduate student health-care plan provided. Maybe, one of my classmates joked, there was something about the nature of our work, at the intersection of different methods and disciplines, neurotically deconstructing the American myth, that predisposed us to this kind of analysis. To me, it seemed like a thing people did on the East Coast, and I was assimilating again. So I made an appointment.

I was telling myself the same story, and I thought a therapist could be an editor of sorts, helping me calibrate the right tone of confessional melodrama. I was shown to a small office in the health building. A woman was seated behind a muted gray desk. Behind her was a bookshelf that felt carefully, warmly curated, a mix of diagnostic manuals, trinkets, and plants. She had red hair and inquisitive eyes. She was not much older than me. I sat down. "My best friend was murdered," I told her. "I went off to a rave, left him on that balcony, and a few hours later he was dead," I continued, still wearing my backpack. "I should have stayed. I could have done something."

She asked me to back up. I offered an abbreviated version of our history. Leaving in the middle of a conversation, my regrets about all those unfinished sentences, the possibility that I was getting laid for the first time as my best friend was dying. Were we best friends? *I'm not sure, actually. Maybe. What does that even mean?* (Takes notes.) I told her about everyone that was there that night, how crazy it was to think that the killers had seen us come and go. *That's crazy, right?* (Slight nod.) I wondered if I had cast a hex by secretly wishing he wouldn't call the next day. (More notes.)

In grad school, I was enamored with things that were impossible to resolve. I studied theory, linguistics, deconstruction, the "worn coin" of truth and language, the formal challenge and underlying ethics of representing rupture, the barbarism of creating art in the shadow of traumatic suffering. All of these lofty ideas appealed to my sense of the world, at least the parts of the readings I understood.

You begin wondering if the stories you tell are false. Whether it would have felt different if it had been this friend who died, rather than that one. You live by worst-case scenarios. That someone who was supposed to call once they arrived at home is actually dead. You google how to access police reports; you punch in a few digits for the nearest police station. You stay up all night, your mind racing, but too afraid to write down your thoughts. You are able to recall with clarity the last time you saw people, what they were wearing, because you are positive that something terrible is about to happen. Something terrible is always already happening. We are always unaware that we already live on the precipice of tragedy. You dwell on questions of potential and promise, what could have been, even as your friend is sitting across from you. Their phone ran out of batteries.

Some days, it was easy to talk, to inflect my voice with a playful lilt. But more often, it felt impossible. I would scramble a simple expression or notice a student looking just past me while I was explaining something, and lose all confidence in my spoken words, and the rest of the day would be spent at home surfing the web or writing emails.

As I described my complicity in Ken's death, the therapist furrowed her brow—a gesture I found unnecessarily aggressive. It was her professional obligation to fix her gaze, never to look away, in order to hold me accountable for what I was saying.

Would it have made a difference? she asked. Did my staying or leaving actually matter? I could have prevented it from happening, I said. She sized me up, likely making the correct assumption about my chances in a street fight. Wouldn't they have just killed both of you? I wasn't sure.

"Why do you think it's your fault?" she finally asked. It had never occurred to me that it was not. Every one of us must feel this way, I said. I was certain. "Do you know that for sure?" Of course. "How do you know that? Have you asked anyone else?" I had not. I assumed we all felt the same way, even if those feelings had metastasized in our bodies in different ways—anger, hate, even a craving for extreme joy.

I'd been afraid to ask anyone else, for I'd long since become the one left behind, shaping my grief into a new persona. She said it wasn't grief but guilt I was holding on to, and that it was pointless to feel guilty, because what could I have done? It kept me in the past. There were three of them and at least one gun. Maybe it was time to let go of that part of the story, she suggested.

It's not as if I had never considered it, but hearing someone else say these things aloud felt invigorating. I'd been writing the same sentences for years, afraid of what might come next. *Therapy is awesome,* I thought to myself; I might have even said it aloud. It was so efficient. We'd been here for only twenty minutes, and I was done. We had ten minutes left for small talk, so I asked her about her interests, what drew her to this line of work, what her other patients were like.

When our session ended, I thanked her profusely. *It was nice knowing you.* But you signed up for an entire semester, she told me, and you should really come back next week. We were just getting started.

I assumed she wanted to continue probing because this was part of her training. And I returned the following week, fearful that I'd be fined. I took off my backpack, hung up my coat, wondered what we could possibly spend thirty minutes discussing this time around. The glow had faded away, but I still felt good. We talked about Ken, and she returned to this question of guilt. She didn't understand why these feelings were so deep-seated. Was I religious? No, I replied, probably the opposite. Were my parents religious? Probably even less so than I was. Religion was one of the few things they were intolerant of. She began speaking more deliberately.

She asked me about my mom and dad. Did they ever tell me they loved me?

No, I said, laughing nervously. *I mean, yes, they do. My parents tell me they love me. I meant no, as in . . . no, they're not the issue here.*

She rephrased her questions about my parents, and I rephrased my answer.

What about pressure? she wondered. Weren't my parents immigrants? Had they put a lot of pressure on me? I mean, here we were at Harvard, after all.

Well, I clarified, *I didn't actually want to be here. I actually wanted to go to NYU, not that that's what you meant. I'm just saying.*

I looked past the deep concern on her face and started reading the spines of the books in her office. Many of them were about the unique psychological makeup of minority students. How-to guides about navigating the emotional landscape of the immigrant experience. Short books about intergenerational conflict and depression. I reminded her I was there for a specific reason. My friend died, and I'm still sad. This has nothing to do with my family.

My parents are great, I said. *Unbelievably non-stereotypical.*

My mom and I were at the mall the summer before I left for graduate school. We were just browsing. I went looking for sneakers and eventually found her sitting on a bench next to an old white woman. As I approached, the woman got up to leave. She smiled softly at me, then looked back at my mom and wished her well. *Who was that?* I don't know, my mom said.

As we walked to the food court, my mom told me that she didn't know the woman but they had started talking. About the weather, the new bakery by Macy's, how much Cupertino had changed. I'm here with my son, my mom explained to this stranger. Something very bad happened to him and his friends. My mom couldn't explain what it was that compelled her to continue telling this person about that night in July. He's sad and I want to help him, she said. I don't know how. I don't know how to talk to him.

She told me all this, and I had no idea what to say, so I said nothing.

As children, we studied our parents' accents wondering how much longer until that suggestion of their old lives disappeared altogether. Their colloquialisms traced back to the season of their arrival—where did my mom learn to say I was "jiving" if I was being unserious? We marveled at how much faster we could speak, and with a clarity that eluded them. It seemed point-less to pass on new idioms, which they always used incorrectly. Writing and speaking were skills we learned on their behalf. But where could it take us?

When I was a teenager, my mom started coming home with

books written by people with Chinese names: autobiographies by doctors, inventors, even a rock journalist; best sellers about families persevering through war and famine, histories of the railroads, gory tales of the Sino-Japanese War; a book of Bill Moyers interviews, because one of the subjects was a Chinese American scholar of Confucianism who taught at Harvard. Evidence that it was possible to appear on the page, even with a name like mine. She had listened quietly to all my dreams and fears, and she was telling me I was not alone. That I would never be alone. But, at the time, I didn't relate to any of these books. I believed I had nothing in common with these people and their stories.

The immigrant's resourcefulness requires an exhaustion of possibilities. You may master tenses and forms, grammatical rules, what passes for style. And yet, consequently, you may struggle to hold a conversation with your grandparents. It's possible they secretly wanted this to happen—a measure of generational progress. The child has learned to speak for himself, but to talk back as well. You write well, not good. The devoted student also internalizes a relationship to the language itself, one in which you remain conscious of your distance from the source, from who draws on this language to mine their authentic self, because you've been led to believe such a thing matters. A simple pronoun of "I" or "we," a first-person perspective, all of it seemed mysterious. We could never write in a way that assumed anyone knew where we were coming from. There was nothing interesting about our context. Neither Black nor white, just boring to everyone on the outside. Where do you even begin explaining yourself?

What I didn't realize at the time was that my therapist wasn't casting aspersions about the hard-driving instincts of Asian immigrant parents. She was asking how I'd become the person sitting in front of her that day. I'd seen the books on her shelf and assumed she was trying to draw out stories that echoed her case studies. But it was less a question of how I was raised than of who my parents were. The horizons they imagined. Who had taught them? Perhaps their parents, too, thought it best to stay industrious and keep your head down.

She was asking, what is history? Do you see yourself in it? Where did you find your models for being in the world? How did you learn about love and honor and pity and pride and compassion and sacrifice? She was looking for turning points. Maybe a feeling, an attitude toward life, a fondness for certain timbres of laughter, the angle of your head as you listened—all the imperceptible qualities that were passed on through lineage. The shape and size of dreams.

Marooned on the East Coast, I drifted further away from my Berkeley friends. I wrote to Ken's parents with less frequency, embarrassed by how much of my own sadness I'd lobbed in their direction, as if they didn't have enough of their own. I felt self-conscious about my grief, and I didn't know how to be a good, present friend.

Whenever I poured old things out of the envelope, sorted them, held them, it was to remind myself of a feeling, to return to some kind of old breathing pattern. But one day I pulled out some photocopies with the words *Barry Gordy's IMBROGLIO* at the top, the script we had written after finding inspiration in *The Last Dragon*. I realized there were more pages than I remembered. Ken had given me a copy of the notes, keeping the original in his notebook. I'd never actually read them.

The plot was straightforward, a boy's infatuation with a girl, the various misunderstandings and travails he must overcome in order to finally see himself. I can't remember if he gets the girl or not. But I do remember thinking that working on the movie was just an excuse to hang out, a way to extend our inside jokes. We would never actually find someone with a camera.

A possible alternate title: *The Losers Club.* The core was Dave ("misunderstood"), Paraag ("ring leader"), James ("steady girlfriend"), Ken, and me. Ken wrote out the film's thematic concerns: "Girls," "Friends," "Parents." I remember when he realized that his expectations for the world, his desire to belong, his belief in chivalry and hard work, had come from the sitcoms we had watched as kids. There's a list of every TV show we could remember, arrows pointing to "white supremacy." In our film, the boy crashes and burns because he's internalized all these lessons, assumed that happy endings are for everyone. He models his behavior after characters on TV, and he has no idea who he really is. In the margins, Ken sketched out a statement of philosophy, riffs and observations around Asian American identity. Quotations from *The Last Dragon*—our canonical text. His grand theories about how we learned to be our authentic selves. Where could we look for models of our American future?

For some reason, he assigned me the role of the boy. In the opening scene, James and I pass by the Campanile, the campus clock tower, and I tell him about a crush. He knows her. He says he'll introduce us, since I lack the necessary social savvy to make anything happen on my own. Sure enough, she appears. I get up to talk to her, but my backpack strap gets caught on the edge of a table, and I tumble to the ground. Awkwardness ensues. The dialogue Ken wrote borrows from our conversations: "there is no such thing as physical attraction," which looked absolutely ridiculous on the page. There's a party scene where my crush vomits in my lap, which leads to digressive bits about "mass culture" and Nietzsche's "On Truth and Lies in a Nonmoral Sense."

I'd forgotten how much of this you bothered to write. I forgot how small your handwriting could be, how it always looked as if your Cs were trying to swallow whatever letters followed. But I do remember watching you write all this down on your legal pad, and how strange it was to realize that you were putting me down in words. The mannerisms and quirks you'd noticed, how you isolated my secret, sarcasm-cloaked earnestness as what was authentically notable about me. And I remember wanting to be more like the person on the page.

About halfway through the script, things get strange. A laugh track appears. There are spoof montages, moments of absurd slapstick. A dinner date goes awry in the most predictable way. I adopt the persona of an asshole because one of my friends tells me that's what girls secretly want. I answer the door dressed like a white dude I'd ridiculed earlier: I'm wearing a Hawaiian shirt and Reef sandals. "Crash into Me" is playing. I offer my date takeout disguised as my own handiwork. Somehow, I cause a kitchen fire, and then I make fun of her concern as we're putting it out. The love of my life decides to go home. "This isn't a sitcom," she says, and a pretaped studio audience goes, "Awwww."

And then you show up. We're studying at a café. You are the cool, skeptical sidekick. (This was definitely your idea.) You're the one always ready with some obscure reference.

You launch into a monologue about how we've been socialized. Where did we learn about the American dream? What role models were available to us? You pontificate on the meaning of Michael Chang. Do the lessons passed down to us by books or movies or TV apply to our lives as Asian kids with Asian parents, or do they make us feel inadequate? Why are we always working so hard, proving our smarts, living up to someone else's standards? Maybe it's all a trap. Why are we looking out for help, when it's all around us? We are not men without a culture. We just have to make it ourselves.

These were our conversations. You were trying to explain where we had come from. How we had learned what it meant to be cool or normal, how we then modeled those poses for one another. The intensity with which we loved and admired our parents, only there were limits to what they could teach us. Who needed role models when we had one another? I didn't understand at that time that you were writing a movie about our own lives. I don't remember whether there was any more than just these pages, or if we stopped working on it altogether, or if you continued on without me. Maybe you stayed dreaming.

You were describing people we had not yet met—maybe people we ourselves would become. Finding a container for all of our jokes, all the dumb things we had seen and done, so we would never forget.

Maybe I would have gone to New York, and not Boston. Maybe I would have gone to Boston, and we would have finally lived together. Maybe it was only a matter of time until we grew apart. We would have continued living, reminded of each other when a song came on during a movie, or on the radio, or whatever unforeseeable technology delivered us beauty. I would have never had a reason to remember all this. Maybe I would not have turned to writing at all. The allure all these years had been the possibility of the asymptote's line one day meeting the curve. At first this realization that I could never force a connection seemed tragic; then it became comforting to imagine that the line and the curve could go on forever. They move in the same direction, even if they never touch.

Maybe, in these other stories I began telling myself, the only writing I'd do would be emailing after a Padres loss. We sign off the same way—*Stay true.* The joke that gave birth to the phrase is lost to time, but I still remember the elaborate handshake that accompanied it. "Stay true to the game," later abbreviated to "stay true." True to yourself. True to who you might have become.

By the end of that semester of free therapy, I was very tired of talking about myself. I was tired of myself. Each week I dutifully showed up, because I was supposed to, and relitigated whatever I had talked about the previous week. Replaying the details of that night demystified it, at least in terms of my involvement. More accurately, noninvolvement, because how could it have ended any differently? That was just the historian trying to wedge himself into a story that was not his.

Talking so much did nothing to lessen the fact that I missed you, and that I could now periodize different eras of that feeling. *I miss missing you circa Oct 98,* I wrote in my journal. *I miss not watching my back, I miss going out for dinner at night, I miss your balcony and cultivating minor league tobacco habits.*

I missed that feeling of having once known exactly what to say. That feeling of writing a series of perfect sentences. In a sense, I was still, years later, stepping down from the podium at the funeral home, shuffling slowly back to my seat in the pews between Anthony and Sean. But this was exactly why Derrida resisted the eulogy form. It's always about "me" rather than "we," the speaker burnishing his emotional credentials rather than offering a true account of the deceased.

The true account would necessarily be joyful, rather than morose, and surrendering to joy wouldn't mean I was abandoning you. A celebration of how it began, rather than a chronicle of free fall, a tribute to that first sip, rather than all the spinning rooms that followed. It would be an account of love and duty, not just anger and hatred, and it would be filled with dreams, and the memory of having once looked to the future, and an eagerness to dream again. It would be boring, because you simply had to be there. It would be poetry and not history.

Our session was nearly up. I told the therapist that she had helped me a lot. The chance to hear myself say these things aloud in a nondescript office building had made me feel utterly ridiculous. I was a legendarily self-involved person. I was always the one to run at the first sign of trouble. What could I have done? But she had helped me rearrange some of the furniture in my mind. I knew what I needed to do now, I told her. I needed to figure out how to describe the smell of secondhand smoke on flannel, the taste of pancakes with fresh strawberries and powdered sugar the morning after, sun hitting a specific shade of golden brown, the deep ambivalence you once felt toward a song that now devastated you, the threshold when a pair of old boots go from new to worn, the sound of our finals week mixtape wheezing to the end of its spool. Which metaphors were useful and which were not, what to explain and what to keep secret. The look when someone recognizes you.

I'm going to write about all this one day, I told her, and she smiled at me.

ACKNOWLEDGMENTS

For the Ishidas. For Anthony, Gwen, and Sammi; Paraag, Sean, and Dave; Derrick, Charles, BMP, Mira, Alec, and Momo. Thanks to all of you for listening, and for all things said and unsaid. For Irami; Ben and Tony; Jen and Rosa; Henry, Zubin, Joe and Sigma Alpha Mu, Grace, Kathy, and Crosley. Thanks to Nate, Eric and *Chinatown,* James, Kiwa, Susie, Ussuri, and Alicia; Ray and Seth; Eddy and the students at San Quentin; Bernice, DHY, and Harish; Rogin; AYP / RYP / REACH!, the Davis zine crew and Regent House, the staffs of *Slant* and *Hardboiled.*

Carol showed me a vision of peace, Zeke a reason for the future. Thanks to Willa, who will never read this. Love transcending language to my family.

This is a book about being a good friend, a term that only occasionally applies to me. The following people are or have been good friends to me, and I am grateful for their camaraderie, belief, and patience: PLO, O-Dub, Jazzbo, Jon, DCT, and Zen; Ed; the Maos; Sonjia; Salamishah, Chinnie, and Rich; Kris and Sarah; Ami; Kirby, Ken, and Herb; Josh and Sarah; Piotr and Kate; Willing, Haglund, Remnick, and Wallace-Wells. Bill H., Jay, Sukhdev, SFJ, Julian, Ross, Paul and Lauren shepherded me around some corners I didn't know were there. Conversations with these people unlocked mysteries for me: Kiese; Scott S.; Mitch, Eric, and Sana; Shinhee; John aka Grand Puba; Cool Chris; Mikey; Amanda; Sake One and Heather. Thanks to my students for teaching me.

I've been writing this for over twenty years. But it didn't become a book until my agent Chris saw it as one. I'm grateful. Thanks, too, to Sarah and the rest of the Gernert Company. I never would have been able to finally write it all down without the support and isolation of the Cullman Center at the New York Public Library. Thomas at Doubleday deserves all the immortalizations. I'm lucky to work with someone who is also now a confidante. One of his strokes of genius was bringing in Oliver, whose design helped me understand something new about my story. Thanks to Johanna, Elena, Lindsay, Cammi, and the rest of the incredible team at Doubleday.